THE SEVEN CHECKPOINTS

Seven Principles Every Teenager Needs to Know

Student Journal

ANDY STANLEY
STUART HALL

HOWARD
PUBLISHING CO.

Our purpose at Howard Publishing is to:

- *Increase faith* in the hearts of growing Christians
- *Inspire holiness* in the lives of believers
- *Instill hope* in the hearts of struggling people everywhere

Because He's coming again!

The Seven Checkpoints Student Journal
© 2001 by Andy Stanley and Stuart Hall
All rights reserved. Printed in the United States of America

Published by Howard Publishing Co., Inc.
3117 North 7th Street, West Monroe, Louisiana 71291-2227

03 04 05 06 07 08 09 10   10 9

Edited by Michele Buckingham
Interior design by Stephanie Denney
Back cover photo by North American Mission Board

Library of Congress Cataloging-in-Publication Data
Stanley, Andy.
   The seven checkpoints : seven principles every teenager needs to know : student journal / Andy Stanley, Stuart Hall.
      p. cm.
   ISBN 1-58229-178-0
      1. Christian teenagers—Religious life. I. Hall, Stuart, 1968– II. Title.

BV4531.3 .S83 2001
248.8'3—dc21   2001024124

Contents

Contents

vi

What's It All About?

The Seven Checkpoints
Seven Principles Every Teenager Needs to Know

seven /se•ven/ *n*: a number that was symbolic in Scripture of completion and perfection.

check /chek/ *n*: a standard for testing and evaluation: CRITERION

checkpoint /chek•point/ *n* (1926): a point at which a check (a standard for testing and evaluation) is performed.

WHAT'S IT ALL ABOUT?

It's a subtle reminder.

Every time I get in my SUV, crank up the engine (and the stereo), and start down the street, I see it. Up there. On the top left corner of the windshield. I can't help but notice it out of the corner of my eye.

No, it's not the small vanilla milkshake that a skillful, dead-aim bird likes to leave me.

It's not the spiderlike crack growing—as if it had a life of its own—from the spot where a rock avalanched out of the back of a dump truck and hit glass.

It's not a pair of fuzzy dice hanging from my rearview mirror. (*Please!* I replaced those with my high school graduation tassels a long time ago!)

No, this *thing* I notice every time I drive my SUV is a clear adhesive sticker that Super Lube places on my windshield each time I have my oil changed. It doesn't particularly jump out at me. It doesn't flash. It isn't neon. But my eye always catches it because I know it's important. That sticker gives me crucial information that will help my vehicle avoid problems and keep running smoothly.

Every time I see that sticker, I am reminded that either *now* or *soon* I will have to take my vehicle back to Super Lube. There I will drive my SUV over a hole in the garage floor, and the Super Lube dudes will give it a complete physical. They will check the air pressure in the tires, check the oil filter and other components under the hood (I have no idea what they all are), change the oil, refill all the fluids in the engine and washer, and more. (By the way, did you know there is a ceiling fan in your car? I learned that from the Super Lube guys. Go see. I promise!)

Sometimes I stand nearby during this process and listen to the guys under the hood and the chassis shouting parts and measurements back and forth to each other. When they find that all is well with a certain part or system, they always call out, "Check!" Finally they hand me their checklist (and my bill). I can review everything that they've done, changed, or replaced, as well as read their assessment of any additional needs my vehicle has.

What would I do without the Super Lube guys? Those regular trips to Super Lube constitute an important checkpoint in my life (and the life of my SUV). Did you notice the definition of *checkpoint* at the beginning of this introduction? For me Super Lube is a checkpoint—a point or place where a standard for testing and evaluating is performed (in this case, on my vehicle).

We all need checkpoints in our lives. We all need to stop and evaluate where we are, how we're doing, and what needs to be done, changed, or replaced to keep us on the right road. The journal you now hold in your hands is designed to be that kind of checkpoint in your life.

The Irreducible Minimum

There are many things you need to know as you grow as a follower of Christ and as a person. But after working with teenagers for twenty years, I am convinced that there are seven principles in particular that all students should understand, commit to memory, and embrace before they leave the safety of their homes and youth ministries. I call them the "seven checkpoints."

These seven student-specific checkpoints are the irreducible minimum. They are the must-know, can't-be-without principles. They are not all that is important. But they are what is most important for you at this stage in your life.

3

These seven checkpoints were developed over time as my staff and I asked some very hard and specific questions that directly involve you:

✔ If we could permanently imprint anything we wanted upon your mind, what would it be?

✔ What do you *need* to know? What is the irreducible minimum?

✔ When everybody else is "doing it," what's going to keep you from joining in?

✔ When you are sitting in a dorm room your freshman year, contemplating your options for the evening, what principles or truths should drift through your mind in that potentially defining moment?

Here's what we came up with:

Checkpoint #1: Authentic Faith

This checkpoint focuses on a correct understanding of faith. Confusion in this one area is the primary reason so many students abandon Christianity. True faith is confidence that God is who He says He is—and confidence that He will do everything He has promised to do.

Principle: God can be trusted; He will do all He has promised to do.
Critical Question: Are you trusting God with the critical areas of your life?
Key Passage: Proverbs 3:5–6

Checkpoint #2: Spiritual Disciplines

The focus of this checkpoint is your devotional life. The apostle Paul says that true spiritual transformation begins with a renewed mind. Only as you begin to renew your mind according to the truths of Scripture will your attitudes and behavior begin to change.

Principle: *When you see as God sees, you will do as God says.*
Critical Question: *Are you developing a consistent devotional and prayer life?*
Key Passage: *Romans 12:2*

Checkpoint #3: Moral Boundaries

One of the most important things you can do as a teenager is to establish clear moral limits. You need to learn how to protect your body and emotions by honoring God's plan for sex and morality. That's the focus of this checkpoint. The depth of your intimacy with God and others depends on it.

Principle: *Purity paves the way to intimacy.*
Critical Question: *Are you establishing and maintaining godly moral boundaries?*
Key Passage: *1 Thessalonians 4:3–8*

Checkpoint #4: Healthy Friendships

The people you associate with the most will have a direct impact on the decisions you make and the standards you choose. Healthy friendships build you up and draw you closer to God; unhealthy friendships bring you down and cause you to compromise what you know is right. This principle focuses on helping you build healthy friendships while avoiding unhealthy ones.

Principle: *Your friends will determine the direction and quality of your life.*
Critical Question: *Are you establishing healthy friendships and avoiding unhealthy ones?*
Key Passage: *Proverbs 13:20*

Checkpoint #5: Wise Choices

This principle focuses on the necessity of applying godly wisdom to the choices you make. Good decision-making is more than simply choosing between right and wrong. You need to learn to ask yourself, "In light of my past experience and my future dreams, what is the wise thing for me to do in this situation?"

Principle: *Walk wisely.*
Critical Question: *Are you making wise choices in every area of your life?*
Key Passage: *Ephesians 5:15–17*

Checkpoint #6: Ultimate Authority

Freedom and authority are often viewed as opposing concepts. But the Bible teaches that true freedom is found under authority. This principle focuses on your need to recognize God's ultimate authority and to respect the earthly authorities He has placed over you.

Principle: *Maximum freedom is found under God's authority.*
Critical Question: *Are you submitting to the authorities God has placed over you?*
Key Passage: *Romans 13:1–2*

Checkpoint #7: Others First

Selfishness comes naturally to us. *Selflessness*, however, must be learned. The Bible says that Jesus "made Himself nothing" in order to serve the people He loved. He put the needs of others ahead of his own. This checkpoint focuses on the true nature of humility and service.
Principle: *Consider others before yourself.*

Critical Question: Are you putting the needs of others ahead of your own?
Key Passage: Philippians 2:3–11

Using This Journal

So how do you use this journal?

Let me encourage you to start each day in this journal by first spending time in worship and prayer. Worship, as my friend Louie Giglio says, is "setting our mind's attention and heart's affection on God." Whether you choose to listen to worship songs, take a walk, or simply sit still in a favorite chair, allow your heart and mind to focus on the Lord. Prayer, or conversation with God, will flow naturally. Simply speak out to God what you think about Him and what you desire from Him that day.

Checkpoint Dilemma

Each week you will journey through one of the seven checkpoints. You will begin your journey by taking a look at a situation or scenario that gives a real-life perspective on why that checkpoint is so vital to your life. I call this the Checkpoint Dilemma. When you read these stories, make sure that you write down, or journal, your thoughts. Highlight places where you can relate. Identify thoughts and feelings that coincide with aspects of the story.

Key Passage

Seven days of devotional readings follow each Checkpoint Dilemma. Each day begins with a key passage of Scripture for you to look up and study. Make sure that you take your time in reading and understanding these verses. Use the following questions to maximize your comprehension and application:

7

✔ What does this passage say? Summarize the scripture in your own words.

✔ Why is this important? Take a guess at why God wants you to know this truth.

✔ What should I do about it? Determine how you can specifically apply this truth to your life.

✔ How can I remember this? Burn the truth on your mind and heart by memorizing the passage, writing it on a card, or asking someone to hold you accountable for its contents.

Questions to Think About

Six questions follow each key passage—three to help you delve into the meaning of the scripture and three to help you think about how it applies to you. Journal your answers to these questions in as much detail as possible. Record your thoughts and struggles as you go along. Don't fly through this part! Schedule enough time to allow yourself to draw out every fiber of meaning God wants you to receive.

More Insight

Following the questions, you'll find a few short paragraphs to give you more insight into the Bible passage as it relates to the checkpoint for that week. The intent is to give your thought processes more "fuel for the fire" and ground you a little more securely in the main principle. Again, make notes, record any questions, and, above all else, journal what you are thinking and feeling as you read.

I can assure you that disciplining yourself to journal your thoughts will serve you well for years to come. Even when you finish this book, don't stop journaling! Keep recording the things you see God doing in your life, your family, and your world. Record the important lessons God is teaching you. Record how you feel about what you see, read, and think. Writing down your emotions is a very healthy habit to practice throughout your life! Your journal will become a written record of your spiritual pilgrimage with the Lord. When you get discouraged or feel that God has left you, you can go back through your journal and remind yourself of His faithful protection, provision, and guidance through the years.

Reading the Gauges

Let's say you just got handed the keys to a brand-new car. You run your hand over the contour, admire the chrome, and give the tires a friendly kick. You open the door and slide into the plush leather driver's seat, taking in a deep whiff of *Eau de New Car*. Next you take a piece of cardboard, cut it to fit the shiny new dashboard, and tape it over the gauges.

Not!

You know what happens to a car when the driver ignores the gauges? It's not a pretty sight! Good intentions and pure motives don't compensate for an empty tank, an overheated engine, or tires that are out of alignment. "But I didn't mean to!" is a lame excuse when you run out of gas in the most dangerous part of town.

The same thing will happen to you if you aren't paying attention to the important gauges in your life. The seven checkpoints in this journal represent some of those gauges. If you don't keep an eye on them, eventually something *will* break down. And it won't be pretty.

I invite you to come with me every day for the next forty-nine days and take a close look at your life's gauges. See where you stand and where you need to

9

stand in relation to each of the seven checkpoints I've identified as the irreducible minimum. Tune out the distractions, focus your heart and mind, and allow God's Super Lube dudes—His Word and His Holy Spirit—to do a total spiritual analysis of your life.

When it comes to your Christian walk, remember this: Those who finish well are not always the smartest, the nicest, or the most spiritual-looking. *They are the ones who paid attention to the gauges.*

10

Checkpoint #1
Authentic Faith
Putting Your Trust in God

Principle
God can be trusted; He will do all He has promised to do.

Critical Question
Are you trusting God with the critical areas of your life?

Key Passage
Proverbs 3:5–6

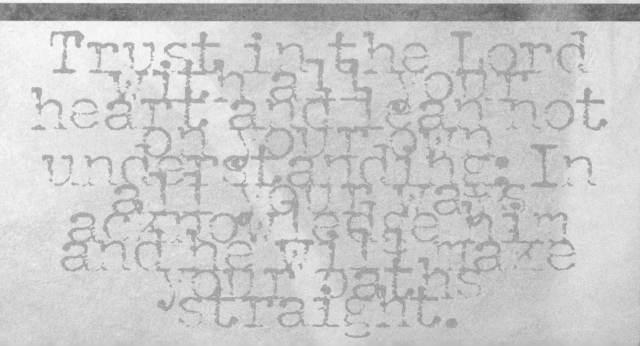

Trust in the Lord with all your heart and lean not on your own understanding. In all your ways acknowledge Him and He will make your paths straight.

Authentic Faith
DILEMMA

Jared is a hard person to figure out. Many of his peers call him two-faced, a hypocrite. Their tainted view of Jared is justified. Even Jared would admit that he is a different person than he was four months ago. Back then, he was active in his church and a leader in his youth group as well as in a Christ-based club at his high school. He was considered a young man of strong faith.

But something happened. Those who don't really know Jared, who don't know about his relationship with Christ, would say that he is just being a normal, fun-loving teenager. Those closest to Jared, however, see that he is spiraling away from God, and they blame it on her.

Jared's about-face seemed to have started when she entered his life. What began as a simple attraction now consumes his attention almost twenty-four hours a day. The high standards Jared once held in regard to dating and girls have gone the way of the dinosaur.

Lauren is having a difficult time believing this whole God thing. It's not because she doesn't want to. In fact Lauren hopes more than anything else that God is real and that He cares. But there are too many unanswered questions, too many tragic circumstances that don't make sense.

It's not that Lauren has never given God a try. She was brought up in church. Her parents were very active in their congregation, and Lauren had no choice but to be in church too. At first she resisted, but as time went on she started to understand how much God loved her. She began to enjoy the worship, the teaching, and the fun she had with her friends there. She received Christ as her personal Lord and Savior, and her faith began to grow.

But the phone call that dreadful night in January literally knocked her to her knees. She couldn't breathe. She couldn't move. In a shower of despair, shock slowly overtook her body and mind. *My mom is dead? She just left the house! Is this a bad dream?*

Lauren never woke from that nightmare. Her mother had been killed in a car accident barely two miles from her home—and God was to blame. If her mom hadn't been so involved at church, she never would have left for the Bible study that night. Surely if God really loved Lauren, her mom would still be alive.

In the process of spiritual renewal and growth, faith is a critical, foundational element. For that reason it is imperative that you understand what faith is and what it isn't. Unfortunately, confusion over the definition of faith is rampant in the Christian community. Often faith is spoken of as if it were some kind of force or power—something you can turn on when you need it—if only you could find the right switch. But that's a faulty definition of faith.

Confusion in this one area is the primary reason so many students abandon Christianity. It is the reason students have such difficulty trusting God with every area of their lives. It is also the reason so many students are unsure of their salvation. Conference after conference, meeting after meeting, camp after camp, they raise their hands again to indicate that they are receiving Christ as their Savior. They're not sure it "took" the last time.

To be a Christian, you must have faith. But what exactly is faith? Let's talk about it.

13

Day One
Circumstantial Faith

14

Read Job 1:6–22

What was Satan implying in verses 9–11 about Job's faith?

_____

_____

_____

_____

_____

List everything Job lost that one day. How would you feel if this happened to you? Explain your feelings. _____

_____

_____

_____

_____

_____

Why do you think Job was able to respond the way he did in verses 20–22?

_____

_____

_____

_____

_____

Think about It

Define _faith_ in your own words. Be as detailed as possible. _____

_____

_____

_____

_____

_____

Was Job's faith based in the present or in something else? What do you think Job's faith was rooted in? _____

_____

_____

_____

_____

_____

_____

_____

How could a good God allow all these bad things to happen to Job? Why didn't God stop the bad circumstances from happening? _____

_____

_____

_____

_____

_____

_____

_____

15

The Old Testament character Job was faced with a series of terrible circumstances that we wouldn't wish on our worst enemy! Fortunately, Job's faith didn't depend on his circumstances. He had faith _despite_ his circumstances.

Circumstantial faith is fragile. It is totally dependent upon our ability (or inability) to interpret events. Kim prays and prays and prays for God to help her pass a test—but she fails. So Kim interprets that failure to mean that God doesn't answer prayer or that maybe He is mad at her. She concludes that God can't be trusted. Her faith is shattered by her interpretation of the circumstances around her.

We are all prone to misinterpret events. Ask a four-year-old being carried by his father into the doctor's office if Daddy loves him. When the doctor brandishes a needle for a tetanus shot, the little boy might have his doubts! But years later, ask that same child about the doctor's visit. He will have a completely different perspective. He will know that his father showed his love by caring enough to protect his son's health.

Just as a child cannot correctly judge his parent's character based on one scary trip to the doctor, so we dare not draw conclusions about God's goodness based upon the immediate circumstances of life. God's faithfulness and loving character do not hinge on the unfolding of circumstances.

Circumstantial faith is fragile because our frame of reference is too small. It is hard for us to look at the significance of events in the context of a lifetime, much less weigh those events on the scale of eternity.

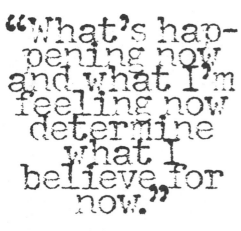

"What's happening now and what I'm feeling now determine what I believe, for now."

Consider Joseph, the boy who spent fifteen years as a slave in Egypt after being sold into slavery by his own brothers. His "tragedy" was a part of a beautiful tapestry that God was weaving behind the scenes to save an entire region from famine. (You can find Joseph's story in Genesis 37–45.) Then there was Moses, the great leader who spent forty years in the wilderness before God sent him back to

16

Egypt—freeing a nation from slavery and unfolding a wonderful purpose in Moses' seemingly purposeless existence. (Read Moses' story in Exodus 2–14.)

For many teenagers, the ever-changing landscape of circumstances defines God. How about you? If God doesn't answer your prayers by next week, do you wonder if He even exists? If you don't see God at work in your immediate circumstances, do you lose your confidence in Him? Do you get stressed out over things like taking a test, getting a date, winning a game, or being left out? (Neutrogena and Oxy10 are making a killing off of your stress!)

Can your faith be summarized by this statement: "What's happening now and what I'm feeling now determine what I believe for now"? If so, you may have a faulty understanding of faith. Are you ready to replace that faulty understanding with an authentic faith? In the spaces below, journal what God is saying to you in regard to your faith. _____

17

_____

_____

_____

_____

_____

_____

_____

_____

_____

_____

_____

_____

Day Two
A Sure Foundation

18

Read Hebrews 4:14–16

When the writer urges us to "hold firmly to the faith," what does that suggest to you? _____

_____

_____

_____

_____

Why does the fact that Christ is our high priest hold so much significance?

_____

_____

_____

_____

_____

_____

_____

This passage seems to imply that the Hebrew Christians had a faulty understanding of the nature of their high priest, Jesus. What were they missing, and why? _____

_____

_____

_____

_____

_____

_____

Think about It

Could you describe the foundation of your faith? Explain. _____

_____

_____

_____

_____

_____

Do you tend to worry and doubt God when bad things happen? Why? _____

_____

_____

_____

_____

_____

Can you think of a time when you nearly abandoned your faith? What happened and why? _____

_____

_____

_____

_____

_____

19

In the book of Hebrews the author addresses a group of Jewish Christians who were being pressured by the Jewish community—and tough circumstances in general—to abandon their faith. Being a Christian seemed to have few practical benefits for these believers. On the contrary, their faith was costing them both socially and financially. Not only were they ostracized in their community, they were banned from the synagogue, which was the hub of their society.

To make matters worse, the Hebrew Christians had been led to believe that Jesus was coming back soon—and thus far He was a big no-show! Now they were beginning to wonder whether or not this Christianity thing was for real.

The author of Hebrews writes this letter to encourage his readers not to abandon their faith. The basis of his argument is the identity of Christ. In the first three chapters, he presents a mountain of evidence pointing toward the conclusion that Christ is God. We believe, he declares, because we know that Jesus walked on this earth, claimed to be God, gave evidence supporting His claim, died for our sin, rose from the dead, and went back to heaven in plain view of hundreds of witnesses. He concludes by stating, "Therefore, since we have a great high priest who has gone through the heavens, Jesus the Son of God, let us hold firmly to the faith we profess" (Hebrews 4:14).

If Christ really is who He says He is, then you don't need to worry when bad things happen to you. You have a high priest who understands. If Jesus really died for your sins, then you have no reason to doubt His love. You have a friend who has laid down His life for you. And if He really meant it when He promised to come back for you, then you don't have to be afraid of what happens next in your life. You have a heavenly Father who has your best interest in mind!

If your faith rests on anything other than the person of Jesus Christ—who He is and what He has done for you—you are building your life on a fragile foundation. Eventually the events of life will sway you to adapt what you believe. Circumstances will cause you to doubt God. But God never intended for your faith to rest upon what's going on around you.

20

Your faith can't rest on your ability to figure out the mysteries of life. It can't rest on your ability to understand how everything fits together. It can't rest on how consistently things go your way or how closely God follows the plans you have made for your life. Your faith can't even rest on whether or not God answers your prayers.

The foundation of your faith must be the person of Jesus Christ. Is that true of you? Record your thoughts in the spaces below. _____

_____

_____

_____

_____

_____

_____

_____

21

If your faith rests on anything other than the person of Jesus Christ—who He is and what He has done for you—you are building your life on a fragile foundation.

Day Three

Faith,
Confidence,
and Wishful
Thinking

22

Read Hebrews 11:1

What does "being sure of what we hope for and certain of what we do not see" mean to you? _____

_____

_____

_____

_____

_____

How can you be sure of something you hope for and certain of something you don't see? _____

_____

_____

_____

_____

_____

_____

Is there a difference between faith and hope? Between faith and confidence?

_____

_____

_____

_____

_____

_____

_____

Think about It

If it were proven to you today that God does not exist, how would your life change? What would you do differently? _____

_____

_____

_____

_____

If Jesus—in the flesh—were to walk in the room you're in right now, what would you do? How would your life change? _____

_____

_____

_____

_____

If faith is being sure of what you hope for and certain of what you don't see, you should be doing the things you say you would do if Jesus were right there beside you. Are you living by faith? _____

_____

_____

_____

_____

Faith is actually a very simple concept. So why are we confused? The answer lies in our unwillingness to accept faith for what it really is rather than what we want it to be. We want faith to be a power that moves God in a direction

23

we have prescribed. We want faith to be the code that unlocks the door to God's unlimited resources—resources we can use at our discretion. Basically, we want faith to be a way for us to get what we want from God.

But biblical faith is not a *force* or a *power*. It is not something we tap into. It is not a tool we use to get something from God. Obi Wan Kenobi ("May the force be with you") is not our leader! That sort of thinking comes dangerously close to New Age philosophy and has no basis in the Bible.

Nor is biblical faith merely *confidence*. When a basketball team bursts out of the locker room pumped up for a game, those players believe they are going to win. If you were to ask the fans in the bleachers if they have faith in their team, they would shout, "Yes!" But that's not biblical faith. That's confidence. The two are not the same.

Biblical faith is also not *wishful thinking*. When we wish for something, we want it, but we have no guarantee that we will get it. If you wrote me after completing this journal and invited me to your house for dinner, would you have faith that I was coming? Would you announce my imminent arrival to your parents? No. You would want me to come, but you wouldn't have faith that I would come. What would it take for you to have faith that I was coming? You would need a letter or phone call confirming the fact that I had accepted your invitation. You would need a promise from me that I would be there. The promise would allow you to move from wishful thinking to faith.

The bridge from wishful thinking to faith is the revelation of God—the wonderful promises He gives

24

> Faith is confidence that God is who He says He is and that He will do all He has promised to do.

to us in His Word, the Bible. God has promised to love you and never forsake you. You don't need to merely wish that He would have your best interest in mind; you can be absolutely confident that He does!

A good working definition of faith, then, is this: *Faith is confidence that God is who He says He is and that He will do all He has promised to do*. It is not confidence in yourself or your pastor or your friends or your circumstances; all these will let you down. It is confidence in the absolute promises and unchanging character of God.

In the rest of chapter 11, the writer of Hebrews gives us dozens of illustrations of people who showed true biblical faith. In every case, that faith was grounded in a promise or a revelation from God. Noah spent 140 years building an ark because God promised that it was going to rain. Abraham left his home and set out without a destination in mind because God promised to lead him to a new home. Gideon charged into an enemy camp totally outnumbered because God promised victory. Moses went back to Egypt and confronted Pharaoh because God promised to deliver Israel through him. Joshua marched around Jericho until the walls fell down because God promised success.

Do you have faith? Does your life reflect your confidence that God is who He says He is and that He will do all He has promised to do? God is trustworthy. Believe it! In the spaces below, let God know the places in your life where you need a promise to have faith. Search Scripture and see if they are there. _____

25

_____

_____

_____

_____

_____

_____

Day Four
The Perfect Father

Read Matthew 7:7–11

Can you explain in your own words what Jesus was trying to say in this passage? _____

_____

_____

_____

_____

Do you think we can ask God for *anything* and receive it? Why or why not?

_____

_____

_____

_____

_____

Does everyone who asks of God receive from God? _____

_____

_____

_____

Think about It

Find one place in Scripture where God says that He will do all that is asked of Him. Write it down. _____

_____

_____

_____

_____

26

Have you ever been guilty of approaching God as if He were a cosmic Santa Claus? _____

_____

_____

_____

_____

Does your faith in God rest on God's doing what you ask of Him—or God's *being able* to do what you ask of Him? What's the difference? _____

_____

_____

_____

_____

27

Let's admit it: We all want to be in the driver's seat. There is something inside each of us that wants a "faith" that puts us in control. I wrestled with this issue as a high school student. I was always trying to find a way, a gimmick, a magic prayer that would force God to do my bidding. But biblical faith puts God firmly in control of our lives. Authentic faith leaves Him with the option to say no.

You must understand this distinction. Only when you come to terms with the true nature of faith will you will be able to surrender your will to God's. The outcome of authentic faith is a life that is in alignment with the will of the Father. As long as you are trying to get something *from* God, you will have a difficult time surrendering your life *to* God.

One of the best things you can do to develop authentic faith is to consistently view God as a perfect father. As my friend Louie Giglio is fond of saying, "God is not a *reflection* of our earthly fathers; He is the *perfection* of our earthly fathers."

Checkpoint #1: Authentic Faith

As a perfect Father, God would not dare give His children everything they ask for. He knows that many of things you think you want so badly are not good for you—in fact, they are downright dangerous to your spiritual life! But because He is a perfect Father, you can always trust Him, even when He seems to act out of character or you don't understand what He's doing. You can be sure that He has your best interest at heart.

Recognizing God as Father is consistent with biblical faith. In fact, Jesus Himself instructed us to address God as "Father." He could have chosen any of a dozen Old Testament analogies for us to use. But He chose for us to call Him "Father." This, then, is how we must view Him!

Because God is our Father, we can ask Him for anything we desire. Jesus assured us in Matthew 7:11 that God loves to give good gifts to His children who ask. We see this love illustrated repeatedly in the Gospels. Often when Jesus healed the blind and the lame, He admonished them not to tell anyone what had happened to them. Apparently Jesus healed these people simply because He, like His Father, enjoyed giving good things to those He loved. He gave because He enjoyed giving.

Today ask God for anything you desire. And as you ask, remember that He is a perfect Father. He wouldn't dare give His children everything they ask for. But He can be trusted to give you good things—simply because He loves you! Spend some time asking God for your desires. _____

_____

_____

_____

_____

_____

Read Proverbs 3:5–6

What does the writer of Proverbs mean by "leaning on your own understanding"? _Depending on your knowledge._

_____

_____

_____

_____

_____

What is the object of faith in this verse? Does the object make it easier or harder for a person to have faith? _Trusting in God is easier._

29

_____

_____

_____

_____

_____

What is the promise in this scripture? _He will make your path straight._

_____

_____

_____

_____

_____

To have authentic faith, we must learn to distinguish between God's promises and our own expectations.

30

Think about It

Is it hard for you to trust God in every area of your life? Why or why not? _____

_____

_____

_____

_____

_____

What is the process you go through to make decisions? _____

_____

_____

_____

_____

_____

_____

The writer of Proverbs says that you should acknowledge God in "all your ways." What does "all your ways" mean in your life? _____

_____

_____

_____

_____

_____

_____

To have authentic faith, we must learn to distinguish between God's promises and our own expectations. There are many things God has not promised that we wish He had. God has not promised to keep bad things from happening to us, for example. God has not promised to heal every illness. He has not promised to reverse the consequences of sin. Yet there are occasions when God intervenes and does all of these things. Why? Because He is a good God who loves to give good gifts to His children.

But He has not promised to do all these things. He is under no obligation. And the fact that parents divorce and grandparents die and friends move away is no reflection on the goodness or presence of our heavenly Father.

But there is a promise attached to authentic faith. You read it in your Scripture reading today: "Trust in the LORD with all your heart…and he will make your paths straight." This promise is one you need cling to with everything you are. Trust in the Lord with all your heart; that is, trust God with every area of your life. He is a perfect Father who can be trusted! And in response to your trust and faith, He promises guidance. Literally, God will make your path—your direction in life—clear and obvious.

God is who He says He is: a perfect Father. And as a perfect Father, He will do all He has promised to do and more. Are there any areas in your life where you need to trust God? Write them down as an act of submission to Him.

31

_____

_____

_____

_____

_____

_____

_____

Day Six
Saving Faith

32

Read Ephesians 2:8–9

According to this verse, what is the element that saves a person? _____

_____

_____

_____

_____

_____

Grace can be defined as God's undeserved favor. How do we get grace from God?

_____

_____

_____

_____

_____

_____

_____

Why do you think Paul emphasizes the connection (or disconnection) between good works and God's grace? _____

_____

_____

_____

_____

_____

_____

Think about It

Do you have a tendency to serve God in order to earn His favor or approval?

_____

_____

_____

_____

_____

Why do you think Paul says we are saved *through* faith and not *by* faith?

_____

_____

_____

_____

33

Is it difficult for you to receive God's grace?_____

_____

_____

_____

_____

_____

_____

Saving faith has a very specific object and a very specific content.

    Faith must always have an object—typically a person or a product. If I told you that I was going to visit you at dinnertime, the object of your faith would be me. If a bar of soap were advertised as being especially good for stopping breakouts, the object of your faith would be the bar of soap. The object of faith is *who* you believe or the *product* you believe in.

Faith must always have *content* as well. When you believe in a product, you believe something *about* the product. You believe it will do what it claims it will do—for example, that the soap will help keep your face clear. Similarly, if you believe in a person, you are confident that the person is trustworthy and will do what he says he will do. You believe, for example, that I will show up at your house for dinner if I say I will. The content of faith is what a person or product promises to do for you. The content of faith is *what* you believe.

Saving faith has a very specific object and a very specific content. The object of saving faith is Jesus—not just God. Jesus said, "I am the way and the truth and the life. No one comes to the Father except through me" (John 14:6).

But what specifically do we need to believe about Jesus? The content of saving faith is like a pair of concrete stakes that must be driven deep into our hearts: (1) Jesus is the son of God, and (2) His death on the cross paid the penalty for all of our sin—apart from anything we do or intend to do to try to "earn" our salvation.

You can believe a multitude of other things about Christ. You can believe that Jesus was born of a virgin, did miracles, died on a cross, and never sinned. The Bible says that each of these is true. But they are not the critical elements of saving faith. The problem with saving faith is not that it is so complex, but that it is so simple!

The way a person comes to salvation is through faith. If you were to ask some friends next Sunday morning why they are at church, they would not answer, "Because of my car!" Their car would be the vehicle that got them to church, but it is not the reason they came. They came to please God and worship with fellow believers. Similarly, faith is the vehicle that carries you to salvation, but Jesus is the reason you are saved. You are saved *through* faith but not *because of* faith.

Salvation is a gift from God. It is not a reward gift. God does not offer it because you deserve it. God offers every person salvation because that is His desire. The way you receive that free gift of salvation is through trusting in God's offer. That is saving faith. It is confidence that God is who He says He is and that He will do all He has promised to do.

Today rest in the fact that God saved you *by* grace *through* faith—just because He wanted to. Spend some time recording your thankfulness for God's grace and your salvation! _____

_____

_____

_____

_____

_____

_____

_____

_____

_____

35

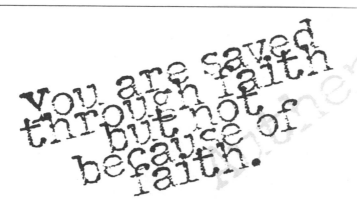

Day Seven
Strength to Endure

36

Reread Hebrews 4:14–16

What are the two things the writer says in verse 16 that you can receive from God? _Grace and mercy._

Does the fact that Jesus can sympathize with your weaknesses have any bearing on what you receive? _____

Why can you draw near to God with confidence? _God will help us when we need it. He can sympathize our weaknesses._

Think about It

What does "mercy" mean to you? _Mercy means kindness and forgiveness._

In this context, what do you think "grace" means? <u>Grace is the strength</u> <u>to endure.</u>

_____

_____

_____

_____

Is there one area in your life where you need strength to endure? <u>studing</u> <u>for tests.</u>

_____

_____

_____

If faith is confidence that God is who He says He is and that He will do all He has promised to do, the question is, What can we expect from God? or, What exactly has He promised us?

The writer of Hebrews says that we can hold firmly to our faith because we have a high priest, Jesus, who has on His own merit "passed through the heavens." He is a high priest who can sympathize with our weaknesses and temptations. Therefore, the writer says, we can draw near to God "with confidence."

"Confidence in what?" you ask. "You've already told me that he may not give me what I want. He might say no. How can I ask for anything with confidence?"

But you *can* approach God's throne with confidence—confidence that He will always give you the two things that are most critical in your time of need: *mercy* and *grace*.

Mercy comes in many forms. Sometimes it is simply the comfort you feel from knowing that, in some mysterious way, you have God's undivided attention when you pour your heart out to Him. At times mercy comes in the form of physical or

> God has not promised to deliver you from your circumstances. He has promised to deliver you through them.

emotional relief. Mercy is the assurance that God will never allow the pressures or heartbreaks of life to be more than you can bear.

You have a Savior who understands. He has felt what you feel. Therefore, He knows exactly what you need. The writer of Hebrews says that you can come to Him with confidence. You can boldly come to God with total transparency and openness. He is never going to say, "I can't believe you did that." He will never respond quizzically, "I can't believe you feel that way." He will never ask emphatically, "What is your problem?" He is a mercy-giving God because He knows from experience what it is like to need mercy.

But God's promises don't end with mercy. You can expect to receive grace as well. In this context grace is the strength to endure, the ability to carry on.

Mom may never understand. Dad may never come back. Your teacher may never lighten up. Popularity may always be elusive. The scholarship may never come through. But God has promised to give you grace—the strength to endure.

God has not promised to deliver you from your circumstances. He has promised to deliver you through them. You have the freedom to ask God to change your circumstances. And you can count on Him for the grace to endure in the meantime.

Ask God in writing to deliver you *through* the circumstances you are in right now. All the tests and violin.

_____

_____

_____

Checkpoint #2
Spiritual Disciplines
Seeing with God's Eyes

Principle
When you see as God sees, you will do as God says.

Critical Question
Are you developing a consistent devotional and prayer life?

Key Passage
Romans 12:2

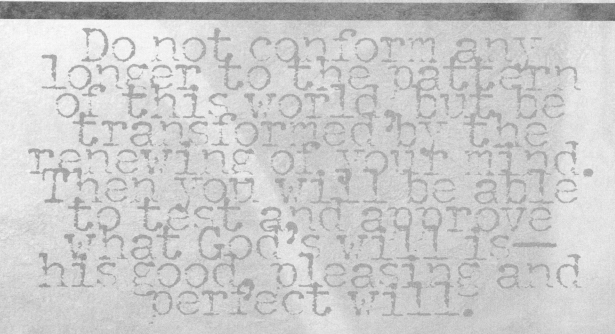

Do not conform any longer to the pattern of this world, but be transformed by the renewing of your mind. Then you will be able to test and approve what God's will is—his good, pleasing and perfect will.

Spiritual Disciplines
DILEMMA

Shaun became a Christian at youth camp last year. He still remembers the feeling of that unbelievable summer night. God seemed to envelop Shaun with His love. People that Shaun didn't even know were hugging him, crying, and talking to him as if they had been friends forever. After he returned from the camp, Shaun continued to feel close to God for a while. He never missed youth group on Wednesday nights, and he even began to talk to his friends at school about their need for a relationship with Christ.

But then it started. The battles with anger, lust, and peer pressure (he always seemed to be hanging out with friends who got him in trouble) began to rage—just as they had before Shaun became a Christian. In fact, the intensity of the battles seemed to be even greater than before.

Then there were the demands of athletics, academics, and other activities that seemed to totally dominate Shaun's time and energies. God and church gradually became less and less important. Shaun's victory in Christ quickly became a momentary retreat from the war. Shaun was once again in the thick of battle, and he was getting slaughtered spiritually.

The good feelings and sense of closeness to God that Shaun felt that summer night slowly but surely faded away. Today Shaun struggles to even go to church, much less feel connected to God. He has made a number of bad choices in friends and activities, and those choices have led to even worse choices and consequences that pain him to even think about.

Shaun is confident that Christ lives in his heart. What he doesn't know for sure is if Jesus can actually change his life the way everyone claims He can.

You will never live a transformed life until you have a transformed mind. You will never have a transformed mind until you have God's thoughts. Spiritual renewal, in its truest sense, is losing your old perspective of life and gaining God's perspective so that you may think and act like Him. It is His perspective, His mind, His thoughts that you need to gain. And you will never have God's thoughts until you begin to experience personal intimacy with God.

How do you do experience intimacy with God and learn to see as He sees? Let's talk about it.

let's talk about it

personal intimacy

His perspective

Spiritual Disciplines

Day One
Renewing Your Mind

Read Romans 12:2

What do you think Paul means when he talks about the "pattern of this world"? _____

_____

_____

_____

_____

_____

According to Paul, what is the key to transformation? _Let your way of_
thinking become different. (changed)

_____

What does "the renewing of your mind" mean to you? _changing your_
mind.

_____

_____

_____

_____

42

Think about It

Think of one area in your life where you tend to continue to sin. What excuses
do you make to rationalize that wrong behavior? What is the lie behind that justification? _____

_____

_____

_____

_____

_____

_____

Think of one area in your life where you tend to overreact. How do you overreact? What is the lie behind your overreaction? _____

_____

_____

_____

_____

Think about your most dangerous temptations—the ones that are the hardest for you to resist. What is the lie behind those temptations? Buying new

clothes. _____

_____

_____

_____

_____

Behavior—both good and bad—is always based on a person's belief system. What you *believe*, or think, shapes your attitudes and determines the way you *behave*, or act.

When Jesus saved you, He changed your identity. Second Corinthians 5:17 says that if you are in Christ, you have become new. But it is your *identity* that has become new—not your *mind*. When you came to Christ, Jesus didn't change your mind. For the most part you still think like you used to, and thus you still behave like you used to. Now your brain has to catch up with your new identity! That is

43

why Paul is so emphatic when he says that true change can only happen when you renew your mind.

I'm reminded of the song "Change Your Mind" by Sister Hazel:

If you want to be somebody else...
If you're tired of losing battles with yourself...
If you want to be somebody else, change your mind.

Spiritual renewal is a process. You must begin to take off the old and put on the new. You must remove the lies that have been inherent in your old way of thinking and replace them one by one with the truth of God's Word. In doing so you are rearranging your belief system—and determining the way you will behave.

That is why spiritual disciplines are so important. By spending time alone with God, praying, and journaling, you can begin to gain God's perspective. And when you start to see things the way God sees them, you will be more apt to do what He says.

Today identify three lies that shape your belief system, write them down, and begin to replace those lies with the truth of God's Word. Be specific. Find Bible verses that directly counter the lies. Be transformed! _____

_____
_____
_____
_____
_____
_____
_____

44

You must remove the lies and replace them one by one with the truth of God's Word.

Read Mark 1:35–37

What do you think was Jesus' reason for getting up so early to spend time with His Father? _He was getting ready to preach._

_____

_____

_____

_____

What was His purpose for leaving the house? _He wanted to pray and_ _be alone._

_____

_____

_____

How are your times alone with God different from Jesus' times alone with God? _Our times aren't everyday and maybe not truthfully._

_____

_____

_____

_____

Day Two

Capturing Time

45

Think about It

Think about the following people from Scripture and explore their stories in the Bible: Moses, Jonah, David, John the Baptist, Paul, and Jesus. What was the one

common denominator in their lives that God used to draw them closer to
Himself? God allowed them to go through an extended
period of solitude before beginning to influence the
World.

Do you struggle with being distracted in your time alone with God? Why or why
not? Yes, I'm always busy.

46

Do you have a consistent time and place where you spend time with God? Why
or why not? No, not alone.

In his book *The Way of the Heart,* Henri Nouwen says, **"Solitude is** the furnace of transformation." Many of the great people in the Bible—Moses, Jonah,
David, John the Baptist, Paul, and Jesus, to name a few—would agree. They all
have a common thread in their history: God allowed them to go through an
extended period of solitude before they began to influence the world. We often
look at their solitude as a time of punishment, but God looked at their solitude as
the perfect environment for transformation in their lives.

Intimacy with God is elusive because it hinges on a fleeting component in life: *time*. Solitude helps you capture time. Solitude pushes out distraction and interruption, giving you more quality time alone with God. Jesus considered solitude important in His time with His Father. So should you. Whenever you can capture time through solitude, that is the time for you to spend intimate moments with the Lord. According to Jesus, the best time is in the morning! But other times are good too.

Do you remember playing hide-and-seek as a kid? Hearing your own heartbeat while you waited for someone to find you? Not daring to move for fear of being found? Your environment of solitude created that sense of quiet, of anticipation, of time standing still. Jesus had a place to go to gain solitude. Do you have a place like that reserved for God?

Solitude will always seem like a waste of time if there is no purpose in it. Solitude without purpose breeds inconsistency and apathy. But solitude with purpose breeds discipline and intimacy. Jesus captured time for one reason: He wanted to experience intimacy with His Father. That should be your goal too.

Today begin to search for your place for solitude. Choose a time to go there. Make it an appointment you wouldn't dare miss! And once you're there, experience intimacy with God. Record what God says to you. That's why He created you. _____

_____

_____

_____

_____

Intimacy with God is elusive because it hinges on a fleeting component in life: time. Solitude helps you capture time.

47

Day Three
Be Still

48

Read Psalm 46:10

Why does the psalmist write "be still" in the imperative form—that is, as a command or necessary action? _____

_____

_____

_____

What do you think he means when he says, "Be still"? _____

_____

_____

_____

_____

Why do you think stillness and knowing God are connected so strongly? _____

_____

_____

_____

_____

Think about It

What is the first thing you do when you get in your car or walk into your room? If I started your car right now, would the radio or CD player come on immediately? _____

_____

Would you say that your heart, mind, and soul are distracted and cluttered? Why? By what? _____

_____

_____

_____

_____

What would you have to change in your life to develop a heart, mind, and soul that are still? _____

_____

_____

_____

_____

_____

Stillness is an attitude.

49

Stillness is not an uncanny ability to keep from moving a muscle. It is not an environment or an arrival point. Stillness is an attitude—a condition of your heart, mind, and soul. It can be summarized in two words: *silence* and *peace*.

In Scripture, peace and stillness mean much the same thing. Paul says in Colossians 3:15 that peace should rule, or have authority, over our hearts. Peace, or stillness, is not a choice; it is a command. This may seem excessive, but the Bible has good reason to stress the importance of stillness. Stillness is imperative to knowing God.

Why? Because God is spirit. The Spirit of God speaks to our hearts internally. More times than not, He speaks softly. You can never connect with the Spirit of God without a heart, mind, and soul that are still!

> # WORSHIP:
> ## our mind's attention and our heart's affection on God.
> —Louie Giglio

Stillness allows you to gain God's perspective on Himself and allows you an opportunity to voice your perspective to Him. Knowing God in this way is the foundation for intimacy with Him. Once you begin to realize who God is, how He thinks, and how and when He acts, you will have no choice but to respond to Him. As you begin to see as He sees, you will want to do what He says.

Stillness also leads to worship. Notice that the psalmist follows the command to be still with the assertion that God will be exalted among the nations and throughout the earth. As I mentioned earlier, Louie Giglio defines worship as "our mind's attention and our heart's affection on God." A distracted mind won't worship. A cluttered heart won't worship. A still mind, however, has no choice but to think of God, and a still heart has no choice but to worship Him.

Today drive to school or work without listening to the radio or talking on your cell phone. Just be *still* in the silence and wait for God to speak. He will. Once He does, use the spaces below to record what He says. _____

_____

_____

_____

_____

_____

_____

_____

_____

50

Read Psalm 119:105 and James 1:22–25

How is God's Word like a lamp in the darkness? _God's word_
lights our way, guides us.

What is the significance to our lives of having a lamp for our feet and a light for
our path? _We will be guided right._

What do you think it means to "look intently into the perfect law that gives
freedom"? Why should we continue to do this? _____

Think about It

Are there any areas in your life in which you need God's light to guide you? List
them specifically. _Yes. Making choices of friends._

Are there any dark areas in your life where you resist allowing God's Word to go? What are they and why? _____

_____

_____

_____

_____

An intimate relationship always hinges on communication.

52

List one specific area in your life in which you continue to resist change. What would you have to do to transform this area of your life? _____

_____

_____

_____

_____

_____

_____

Throughout history the Bible has been used as a history book, a source for debate, and justification for such acts as murder and war. Clearly, God's Word means a lot of things to a lot of people. Very few people view God's Word as what it is—His love letter to us.

An intimate relationship always hinges on communication. It is not enough that you talk to God in prayer; He must talk to you. He must have an equal voice in His relationship with you.

Everything in Scripture is God's communication to you. You must fall in love with God's Word if you want to have intimacy with Him. If you don't exchange communication with God, your relationship with Him will be like the two love-crazed freshmen on the phone at 3:00 A.M., sitting in silence until one says, "I love you," and the other replies the same. That is neither communication nor intimacy.

Why do many of us resist reading and getting to know the Bible? Because it tends to illuminate the dark places inside of each of us. God's Word is active, alive, penetrating, and judging. Hebrews 4:12 likens it to a double-edged sword that "penetrates even to dividing soul and spirit, joints and marrow; it judges the thoughts and attitudes of the heart."

But God's Word also directs us through the darkness. I have an oil lamp from the Holy Land that is smaller than the palm of my hand. In Bible times people used this kind of lamp at night to make their way through the darkness. Many scholars believe this is this type of lamp that the writer was referring to in Psalm 119:105. It only gives out enough light for you to see a few feet in front of you—but that's all you need to hold God's hand and take one step at a time.

Many of us are guilty of reading the Bible but not doing what it says. That's not communication! Imagine me listening to my wife complain about being sick and doing absolutely nothing to help. Or hearing her say that she loves me and simply staring off into space. We have a tendency to take the old saying, "Don't just sit there…do something!" and reverse it to say, "Don't just do something…sit there!"

You would never look in a mirror, see some things out of place, and not make the necessary changes before leaving the house! In fact, you probably get up early just to make sure you have time to make those changes. Many of us have discipline—just not in the most crucial area of our lives, our relationship with God. His Word is like a mirror. When we look into it and see changes that need to be made in our lives, we would be foolish to simply walk away.

53

Checkpoint #2: Spiritual Disciplines

To be a doer of God's Word and not just a hearer, discipline yourself to answer four key questions every time you read the Bible:

- ✔ What does this passage say?

- ✔ Why is this important?

- ✔ What should I do about it?

- ✔ How can I remember this?

Today pinpoint the places in your life where God's Word can give you guidance. Find the appropriate scriptures and shine His light there. Ask the four key questions. Specify where you need transformation and let the reflection of His Word begin to change you. Write it down! _____

_____

_____

_____

_____

_____

_____

_____

_____

_____

_____

_____

_____

Day Five

God's Duct Tape

Read Psalm 119:11 and Colossians 3:16

What does the psalmist mean by "hiding" God's Word in our hearts?

_____

_____

_____

_____

What critical reason does he give for hiding God's Word in our hearts? _____

_____

_____

_____

_____

What do you think Paul means when he challenges us to "let the Word of Christ dwell in [us] *richly*"? _____

_____

_____

_____

_____

55

Think about It

Compare the lyrics to some of the popular songs you know with the things Jesus said in the Bible. Why is there such a distinct difference? _____

_____

_____

_____

_____

Checkpoint #2: Spiritual Disciplines

Do you consider Scripture memorization an important element of your faith? Why or why not? _____

_____

_____

_____

_____

_____

How much time do you spend meditating on God's Word? What does meditation mean to you? _____

_____

_____

_____

_____

_____

_____

_____

When a lady wants to change her fingernail polish, she goes through a process of removal. First she uses fingernail polish remover to take off the old polish. Then she applies the new polish.

As we said in Day One, spiritual renewal is a process of taking off lies and putting on truth. You must do both; to do one but not the other leaves a mess. Two critical elements of this process are *memorizing* God's Word and *meditating* on it in your times alone with God. Through these disciplines you uproot sinful lies planted in your old way of thinking and replace them with God's truth.

Scripture memorization is the discipline of remembering God's Word—of hiding His Word in your heart, as the psalmist says. Meditation is the discipline of thinking on and applying God's Word. Meditation is not a trancelike state of being. It is a train of thought. It is the process of knowing what God says and thinking about how to put it into practice in your life.

I'm reminded of duct tape—you know, that thick, black, sticky tape that keeps things together seemingly *forever*. No home should be without a roll of duct tape! Scripture memorization and meditating on God's Word are God's duct tape for your life. They keep God's mind and heart stuck tight to your mind and heart.

Some people memorize song lyrics. Others memorize commercial jingles. People tend to memorize and learn what they want to memorize and learn. But only God's Word replaces lies with truth. Today begin to memorize and meditate on the Word of God. Hide it in your heart!

In the spaces below, record your thoughts about memorizing Scripture.

57

_____

_____

_____

_____

_____

_____

Spiritual renewal is a process of taking off lies and putting on truth. You must do both; to do one but not the other leaves a mess.

Day Six
Conversing with God

58

Read Matthew 6:9–13

Does it ever bother you that God is untouchable and in heaven? Explain your answer. _____

_____

_____

_____

_____

What does it mean to consider something "hallowed"? _____

_____

_____

_____

_____

_____

What did Jesus mean when He asked God to "give us today our daily bread"?

_____

_____

_____

_____

_____

Think about It

Rewrite Matthew 6:9–13 in your own words. Be as detailed as possible. _____

_____

_____

_____

_____

_____

_____

_____

Would you consider yourself someone who has a strong prayer life? Why or why not? _____

_____

_____

_____

What does prayer mean to you? Explain your answer. _____

_____

_____

_____

_____

_____

Prayer is our conversation with God—our part of the intimate relationship that God longs to have with His children. Because Jesus died for our sins, we can enter into God's presence with confidence, knowing that He hears us and wants us to converse with Him.

"The Lord's Prayer," as this passage in Matthew 6 is known, is how Jesus Himself encouraged His disciples to pray. We all could use a lesson in prayer. Let me encourage you to pray in three ways:

59

Because Jesus died for our sins, we can enter into God's presence with confidence, knowing that He hears us and wants us to converse with Him.

1. Pray through the verse or passage of Scripture you read each day.

Using Matthew 6:9–13 as an example, you could pray like this: "Lord, thank You for being my Creator; You are worthy of my praise. Help me to seek Your will and do Your will every day. Help me to forgive as You have forgiven me.…"

2. Pray through your day.

Think about all the things you will be doing today and pray like this: "Today I will be tempted to _____. Give me strength to resist. This afternoon I am meeting with _____. Help me to show love. Today I need to talk to _____. Open his heart to hear the gospel."

3. Pray through your relationships.

Pray for your family, your friends, your teachers, and your acquaintances. You may find it helpful to pray in concentric circles. That is, begin by praying for the people and matters that are closest to you. They represent your inner circle. Then move outward, praying for people and things that are of lesser concern.

Today begin to pray through the Scripture, through your day, and through your relationships. Don't merely develop a prayer life. Develop a praying life! Record your prayers today in the spaces below.

_____

_____

_____

_____

_____

_____

Read 1 Timothy 4:7–8

What do you think Paul means when he says you should "train yourself to be godly"? _____

_____

_____

_____

_____

_____

In what ways do you think godliness has "value for all things"? _____

_____

_____

_____

_____

_____

How does godliness hold promise for both the present and the future? _____

_____

_____

_____

_____

_____

Think about It

How have the past six days been like spiritual training for you? _____

_____

_____

Day Seven
Recording
Your Progress

61

Checkpoint #2: Spiritual Disciplines

What are the areas in which you are spiritually weak and need to grow stronger?

_____

_____

_____

_____

_____

Have you developed the spiritual disciplines of time alone with God, Scripture memorization and meditation, and prayer? Which of these are habits for you? Which of these are you weak in? _____

_____

_____

_____

_____

_____

Do you have a written record or journal of your spiritual progress? How would such a record be helpful? _____

_____

_____

_____

_____

_____

_____

Spiritual disciplines are not easy to develop. Capturing your time through solitude, developing an attitude of stillness, beginning the process of renewal by memorizing and meditating on Scripture, and being in constant conversation with God takes a lot of energy and focus.

Developing these disciplines, however, is the key to experiencing intimacy with God. As your spiritual habits begin to take root, you will begin to see the fruits of your labor and experience new depths in your relationship with Christ. You will begin to see as God sees. You will begin to do what He says. Your love story with God will become a never-ending, always-deepening, forever-growing saga of His love and grace in your life.

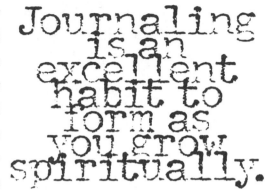

Journaling is an excellent habit to form as you grow spiritually. A journal is a written record of what God has taught you and accomplished in your life. Chuck Swindoll calls journaling "an intimate record of the journey that the Lord and I are traveling on." Did you know that when you read the book of Psalms, you are reading a portion of King David's journal?

63

The purpose of journaling is to record the progress you're making on your spiritual pilgrimage. It must be a weekly, if not daily, habit. You will write things down in your journal that you wouldn't express anywhere else—things like:

✔ **what you see God doing in your life, your family, and your world**

✔ **the important lessons God has taught you and continues to teach you**

✔ **how you're feeling at a certain moment in time**

Looking back is the only way to know how far you have come. I started keeping a journal when I was seventeen years old. Now when I am discouraged or think God has abandoned me, I do a quick review of my journal to remind myself that God is intimately and actively involved in my life.

Today spend some time recording everything that God has done in your life through these seven days of exploring spiritual disciplines. Begin the habit of journaling. You will be glad you did! _____

_____

_____

_____

_____

_____

_____

_____

_____

_____

_____

_____

_____

Looking back is the only way to know how far you have come.

Checkpoint #3

Moral Boundaries
Paving the Way for Intimacy

Principle
Purity paves the way to intimacy.

Critical Question
Are you establishing and maintaining godly moral boundaries?

Key Passage
1 Thessalonians 4:3–8

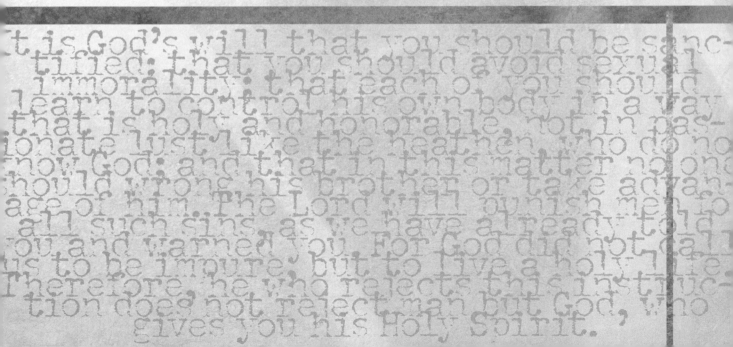

It is God's will that you should be sanctified: that you should avoid sexual immorality; that each of you should learn to control his own body in a way that is holy and honorable, not in passionate lust like the heathen, who do not know God; and that in this matter no one should wrong his brother or take advantage of him. The Lord will punish men for all such sins, as we have already told you and warned you. For God did not call us to be impure, but to live a holy life. Therefore, he who rejects this instruction does not reject man but God, who gives you his Holy Spirit.

Moral Boundaries
DILEMMA

I will never forget my conversation with a woman who came to see me years ago. At that time Jenny was in her early thirties and had been divorced for eight years. She had only been a Christian for about six months. As soon as she sat down, she said, "I have two questions. The first one is about the church, and the second one is personal."

I honestly can't remember her first question. But her second question is forever etched in my memory. She looked me right in the eye and said, "OK, about sex. Does the stuff in the Bible about sex being only for married people apply to somebody like me, or is it just for teenagers?"

At first I didn't know what to say. I knew what I believed, but I wasn't sure how to communicate it. Jenny noticed my hesitation. She went on to explain that since she had been married before, she wasn't sure if she was expected to remain celibate. From her perspective, not having sex seemed like an unreasonable expectation.

I stalled as long as I could. She deserved an answer. But I knew her faith was new and still quite immature. I was just about to launch into my "sex is for marriage only" sermonette when a question suddenly popped into my mind. To this day I believe God rescued both of us by turning my thoughts and words in a different direction.

I looked at Jenny and said, "Before I answer that question, let me ask you a question. Has sex outside of your marriage made your life better or just more complicated?"

She dropped her head and stared at the floor for a moment. Then she began to cry. Through sobs, she forced out her answer: "More complicated."

I waited for a minute before I said gently, "Jenny, that's why God has reserved sex for marriage."

If I could drill one principle into the minds and hearts of students when it comes to sex, it would be this: Purity paves the way to intimacy. When I encourage kids to wait until marriage to experience sex, I am really asking them to remain pure. The question that must be answered then is, Why remain pure?

What's the advantage of purity? What do you gain by remaining pure that is better than what you give up?

The answer is simple: intimacy. Intimacy is the joy of knowing someone fully and being known by them with no fear of rejection. Purity paves the way for intimacy. Impurity, on the other hand, erodes the capacity to experience intimacy—and consequently diminishes the satisfaction of sex.

Not sure you believe me? Let's talk about it.

67

Day One
Pursuing Intimacy

68

Read 1 Corinthians 6:18

How would you define "sexual immorality?" _____
_____
_____
_____
_____

How does Paul encourage us to deal with sexual immorality? _____
_____
_____
_____
_____
_____

Why do you think sexual immorality is a sin against your own body? _____
_____
_____
_____
_____
_____

Think about It

What do you gain by remaining pure? _____
_____
_____
_____

How does what you gain by remaining pure compare to what you give up if you don't?_____

_____

_____

_____

_____

In your own words, define *intimacy*. _____

_____

_____

_____

_____

_____

Sexual purity paves the way to intimacy.

69

Intimacy is the incredible joy of knowing someone fully and being known by them with no fear of rejection. It is a wonderful thing, something to be desired. But intimacy is fragile. It doesn't just *happen*. And it can be destroyed.

Sexual purity paves the way to intimacy. On the other hand, sexual impurity erodes a person's capacity to experience intimacy.

Men and women who've had affairs admit that even if they've been able to hold their marriages together, they can never achieve the intimacy they once had with their spouse. The impurity of their sinful actions has damaged their ability to be intimate. They can no longer be sure that they are knowing and being known without fear of rejection.

There is no escaping this principle. When people involve themselves sexually outside of marriage, they damage their capacity for intimacy.

When you sin sexually, you sin against yourself; you hurt yourself. You damage your potential for a satisfying sexual relationship with a marriage partner down the road. You rob your future spouse of intimacy as well. Perhaps this is why Paul says that sexual immorality is unique; its devastating impact not only hurts you, it hurts your future husband or wife.

You don't really want sex. What you want is intimacy. You want to meet a guy or girl, fall in love, and know that you can trust that person completely. You want to share everything there is to know about you without fear of betrayal or rejection. You want to know that person fully and be fully known. What you are after is intimacy, not sex!

Many young people are afraid of marrying someone and then losing the attraction for that person. They don't want to feel stuck. The best way for you to ensure that you don't lose "that loving feeling" with your future spouse is to set your sights on intimacy rather than sex. Great sex is the by-product of maximum intimacy. And purity now paves the way for intimacy later on.

In the spaces below, record your thoughts regarding today's journal entry.

_____

_____

_____

_____

_____

_____

_____

_____

Read 1 Thessalonians 4:3–8

What does Paul mean by being "sanctified"? _____

_____

_____

_____

_____

_____

What three things does Paul say are God's will for you in sanctification? _____

_____

_____

_____

_____

_____

What does Paul mean by "wronging" a brother as it relates to sexuality? _____

_____

_____

_____

_____

_____

Think about It

Is having sex a biblical concept? _____

_____

_____

_____

Day Two
Uniquely One

71

Checkpoint #3: Moral Boundaries

What is the most difficult aspect for you personally of waiting until marriage to have sex? _____

_____

_____

_____

_____

Do you think God wants to make you miserable by making you wait? _____

_____

_____

_____

_____

72

Simply "having sex" is not only unbiblical, it is impossible! When two people come together sexually, they become one flesh. They are united. In other words, sex is not just physical. There is more to it than that.

Sex was designed by God as an expression of intimate oneness in body that matches a couple's commitment to oneness in purpose and direction in life. That means that each of us is designed to become one with only one other person. When someone participates in sex outside of marriage, that person forfeits the opportunity to become uniquely one physically with their husband or wife. Every time a teenager has sex before marriage, that student decreases the significance of sex with his or her future partner. The oneness factor is damaged before it even exists.

> Sex was designed by God as an expression of intimate oneness in body that matches a couple's commitment to oneness in purpose and direction in life.

The question you must strive to keep in the forefront of your thinking is this: *Are the temporary pleasures derived from sex worth the long-term complications it can cause?* My experience as a counselor and pastor has convinced me that the pain caused by sex before marriage far outweighs the pleasure. The pleasure is for a moment. The pain can last a lifetime.

God knows all of this. That is why His will for you is abstinence. To be sanctified means to become like Christ in your character. That is God's design for you. He wants you to become like His Son. God's will for you in relation to sex is to wait.

Why? Because God wants you to be miserable? On the contrary, it is because God loves you and wants the best for you. It is because God wants your sexual experience to be the best it can possibly be. And He knows more about good sex than anyone does.

God is not against sex. He created it. God is not against you. He created you. And God is not against your having sex. But He wants you to wait.

Sex is not for mature people. Sex is not for ready people. Sex is not for in-love people. Sex is for *married* people. Why? Because sex is not just physical; it is relational. It is to be reserved for the unique, committed, multifaceted relationship of marriage. Only between man and wife can sex be the wonderful and intimate experience that God always intended.

Write down the places in your life where you need to be sanctified and ask God to help you get there! _____

_____

_____

_____

_____

God is not against sex. He created it. God is not against you. He created you. And God is not against your having sex. But He wants you to wait.

73

Day Three
Developing Relationships

Read Genesis 2:21–24

What is the significance of Eve being created from Adam's rib? What does this passage say must happen before a man and woman become "one flesh"? _____

_____

_____

_____

_____

Who are "they" in verse 24? Is the author just talking about Adam and Eve?

_____

_____

_____

_____

_____

_____

Think about It

Do you think this first account of sexuality was purely physical? Why or why not?

_____

_____

_____

_____

_____

74

Why do sex and intimacy go together? _____

_____

_____

_____

_____

_____

According to these verses, what was the original purpose for sex? _____

_____

_____

_____

_____

When Adam and Eve had sexual relations, they didn't just "have sex." Something much more significant happened. They became one flesh. Through those intimate moments together, they were united.

The reason satisfying sex and intimacy go together is because sex is not just physical, it is relational. Unfortunately in our society sex is almost never talked about or portrayed in the context of long-term relationships. Movies, television, magazines, and popular music have ripped sex out of its relational context. But God says sex is highly relational. And when you take sex out of its relational context, you will have problems. There will always be consequences. Sex for the sake of sex will always be less than satisfying.

Since sex is relational, you need to direct your attention to developing great relational skills rather than pursuing sexual experiences. Sexual experience now does not translate into sexual fulfillment later on. In fact, as we've said, the very opposite is true.

The best thing you can do now to ensure a good relationship with your husband

75

The best thing you can do now to ensure a good relationship with your husband or wife later on is learn how to honor and respect the women and men God has put in your life—namely, your mom, dad, brother, and sister.

or wife later on is learn how to honor and respect the women and men God has put in your life—namely, your mom, dad, brother, and sister. As strange as it may sound, the best way for you to prepare for a great sex life later is to learn how to love your mom or dad now! Why? *Because great sex is the by-product of a great relationship.* And relational skills aren't magically embedded at the altar. They are learned over time.

In all your relationships, shift your focus from the physical to the relational side of the equation. If you are willing to do this, you will have a much greater chance of keeping the physical and the relational in proper balance. The relationship skills you develop now will serve you well—with your future marriage partner and for the rest of your life.

Would you say you have great relational skills? Be specific and record the areas where you need improvement relationally. Ask God on paper to help you. _____

_____

_____

_____

_____

_____

_____

_____

Read Proverbs 28:26 and Ephesians 5:15

Day Four
Drawing the Line

How do these verses challenge you in relation to your sexuality?

_____

_____

_____

_____

Why is trusting in yourself foolish? _____

_____

_____

_____

_____

What is the promise for those who walk in wisdom? _____

_____

_____

77

Think about It

When it comes to physical involvement with the opposite sex, does Scripture draw an absolute line saying how far you can go without going too far? _____

_____

_____

How do *you* determine how far is too far? _____

_____

_____

_____

_____

Checkpoint #3: Moral Boundaries

What is the key, in your opinion, to being wise with moral boundaries? _____

_____

_____

_____

_____

_____

When it comes to physical involvement with the opposite sex, the Bible does not give us a specific answer to the question, "How far is too far?" To walk in purity, the question you must learn to ask yourself is, What is the wise thing for me to do? Choosing the way of wisdom is always the safest path to take.

Common sense is one facet of wisdom. Here are four common-sense principles you should commit to memory as you wrestle with the question of how far is too far:

1. The further you go, the faster you go.

On the continuum that moves a couple from the starting point of "Hi, my name is _____" to the culminating point of sexual intercourse, there are many transition points. Understand that every time your physical involvement with a person passes through one of those transition points and moves to a new level, your sense of fulfillment won't last as long as it did at the previous level of involvement. Desire accelerates. It never slows down.

2. The further you go, the further you want to go.

Your sexual appetite is somewhat like your appetite for food. It is never fully and finally satisfied. When you feed an appetite, you increase both its capacity and its intensity. If you have ever tried to eat half of a dessert, you know what I mean. It is easier not to eat any at all! The more you eat, the more you want to eat.

When it comes to sex, drawing a boundary line mentally does nothing to stem your desire physically. You will always want to go further. Short of intercourse, there is no "ultimate" satisfaction. Our bodies were designed to go "all the way." The only way to keep your sexual appetite in check is to not keep feeding it more.

3. The further you go, the harder it is to go back.

God did not design you to go back. He designed you to move forward sexually. Consequently, it is almost impossible to permanently retreat to safety once certain lines have been crossed.

4. Where you draw the line determines three things.

✔ *The arena of your temptation.* If you decide that the line for you is kissing, then you have determined what you will be tempted to do next—namely, whatever you perceive the next step to be after kissing. If you decide that oral sex is OK, then you have determined the arena of your next temptation as well. Every conviction has a corresponding temptation. When you set your standards, you also determine your temptation.

✔ *The intensity of the temptation.* Temptation increases with increased passion, and passion increases as a couple moves closer and closer to intercourse. Every couple is going to be tempted. Assuming you will be tempted to go further than you choose, how intense do you want that temptation to be? Where you draw the line determines the intensity of the temptation. You are actually choosing the level of pressure you will feel in your dating relationships.

79

✔ The consequences of giving in to temptation. If a couple has decided that holding hands is far enough, and one night after a romantic date at Steak and Shake they get carried away and actually kiss, what are the consequences? A touch of guilt, perhaps. Worse case scenario, somebody gets strep throat. But if a couple has drawn the line at the edge of intercourse...you get the picture.

You are in a sense determining your own destiny by choosing where you draw the line. From time to time passions will run high, and even the strongest Christian may temporarily allow his or her standards to slip. Where you have drawn the line will determine the nature of the consequences once that line has been crossed.

Too far, then, becomes your desire for holiness coupled with the tool of wisdom. Both can only be elevated in your life when truth is elevated in your life. And when that happens, the too-far line becomes too high to jump over!

Do you struggle with the issue of "How far is too far?" Write down your thoughts, struggles, and needs to God in the spaces below. Be specific!

_____

_____

_____

_____

_____

_____

_____

80

You are in a sense determining your own destiny by choosing where you draw the line.

Day Five
What's Your Story?

Read Matthew 7:24–27

What were the two things that deemed the first man wise? _____

_____

_____

_____

_____

What did Jesus compare doing these two things to? _____

_____

_____

_____

Contrast verse 24 with verse 26. What is the one obvious difference between a wise man and a foolish man? _____

_____

_____

_____

_____

Think about It

Have you ever thought about your dating habits and relationships as the foundation for your marriage? Why or why not?_____

_____

_____

_____

If you had to build a marriage on your dating foundation today, would it be a strong or weak structure? _____

81

What areas of the foundation need strengthening? _____

_____

_____

_____

_____

_____

_____

    The whole "How far is too far?" question is so confusing. It doesn't help that you are immersed in a culture that thinks the question is bogus to begin with. The issue for most of your friends is "How far *can* I go?" not "How far *should* I go?"

    When I was moving through the maze of adolescence, a different question brought this whole issue into focus for me: How far would I want my future wife to go with the person she dates right before meeting me? I really hated that question. It may have been difficult for me to determine how far I should go sometimes, but I knew exactly how far the person I would one day marry should go: not very far.

    Someday you will probably meet someone you will want to spend the rest of your life with. When you do, you will have one of three stories to tell:

Story One

    When I was a teenager I messed up sexually. I got carried away with the person I was dating. I figured that since I did it once, it really didn't matter if I did it again. So I slept with several other people along the way to meeting you.

82

> How far would I want my future wife to go with the person she dates right before meeting me?

Story Two

When I was a teenager I messed up sexually. But when I was _____ years old, after hearing my youth leader teach on moral boundaries, I decided that God knew what He was talking about. Sex was created for marriage. I decided that from that point on I would wait. I set new standards and have stuck with them. Since that day I have saved myself for you.

Story Three

When I was a teenager I realized that God knows more about sex than anyone. Since He created sex for marriage, I decided to wait. I have saved myself for you.

Which story will you tell? If you already are living with the guilt and regret of having gotten too involved sexually, allow me to reassure you of God's grace and forgiveness. Regardless of what has happened in the past, you can begin again. The fact that you have gone too far is no reason to give up the fight and give in to temptation.

Make a decision today. Whether you have gone too far or not, you can determine that from this point on you will save yourself for your future mate.

Tell God in the spaces below what you want your story to be. Ask Him to help you live up to what you want! _____

83

_____

_____

_____

_____

_____

_____

_____

Day Six
Don't Believe It

84

Read Proverbs 4:23

According to this proverb, how high a priority should you place on guarding your heart? _____

_____

_____

_____

_____

Why is guarding your heart so important? _____

_____

_____

_____

_____

_____

What do you think the writer means by "the wellspring of life"? _____

_____

_____

_____

_____

_____

Think about It

Do you effectively guard your heart? How? _____

_____

_____

_____

How has a lack of guarding your heart affected your wellspring of life? _____

_____

_____

_____

_____

What specific areas of the wellspring of your life need guarding? _____

_____

_____

_____

_____

As you strive to guard your heart, you must be wary of the one-sided messages society continually sends you. Here are six themes that are overtly and covertly woven into the culture, entertainment, and literature aimed at students:

1. Everybody is having sex.

To begin with, that is not a true statement. Secondly, it is not an argument for or against anything. It is simply a statement. The fact that everybody is doing something is not an argument in favor of that something. Because someone else does or does not do something is not a reason for you to do or not do it. Those who are not having sex don't talk about it. There is nothing for them to talk about. There is a silent majority among your peers.

2. You can't live without sex.

Nobody says this directly, but it is certainly implied in much of the music of our culture. One young lady told me that she assumed her boyfriend was having

85

sex with somebody somewhere since she wouldn't sleep with him. It may come as a shock, but no one has ever died from *not* having sex. Yet thousands of people have died from AIDS and other sexually transmitted diseases (STDs) as a result of their sexual activity.

3. Sex is a natural part of a loving relationship.

If this is true, why can't those students who are so sexually active maintain long-term, loving relationships? Instead of sex making the relationship better, it drives a wedge between the two parties. If you want to know about real, fulfilling, long-term, loving relationships, find someone who has one and ask that person about it.

4. Sex is a natural part of growing up.

The truth is, sex *keeps people from* growing up. Our culture argues that the more sexual experiences you have, the more grown-up you become. On the contrary, nature itself tells us it is not natural to have multiple sex partners. There are more than fifty types of venereal diseases that have been identified to date. Many are treatable but incurable. Some can even kill. Not only is it not natural to have multiple sex partners, it's not a healthy way to grow up.

5. Sex outside of marriage would cease to be a problem if teens would just wear condoms.

This widely held myth is the clearest indication that our society has divorced sex from intimacy and relationship. Everyone is warning students about the physical consequences of unprotected sex. Nobody is warning them about the emotional and relational consequences.

The message society sends is that the only problems related to sex before marriage are disease and pregnancy. But condoms do nothing to block the mental and emotional consequences of sex.

- ✔ A condom can't erase a memory.

- ✔ A condom can't remove guilt.

- ✔ A condom can't restore your reputation.

- ✔ A condom can't repair your self-esteem.

6. Sex makes life better.

The truth is, sex outside of marriage doesn't make life better. It makes life more complicated. Every day of your life you are told that sex can have physical consequences. What you never hear is that there are emotional, mental, and relational consequences as well. No one escapes. These consequences will follow you into one relationship after another and will ultimately impact your marriage.

Fire in the fireplace is a wonderful thing. Fire on the carpet, however, can burn down your house. Sex is like fire. In the right context, it is awesome. But when it is outside the context it was designed for, sex can burn your life and your relationships to the ground. Don't play with fire!

Which of these lies do you have a tendency to struggle with? Be honest with God in the spaces below about your struggles. _____

_____

_____

_____

_____

87

Day Seven
A Great Idea

88

Read Psalm 119:9–10

According to this passage, how can a young man (or woman) keep his or her way pure? _____

_____

_____

_____

_____

_____

How desperate was the psalmist for purity? _____

_____

_____

_____

_____

_____

The word translated here as *pure* means "free from all moral taint." Could that definition characterize your life? _____

_____

Think about It

Do you have clear moral boundaries? _____

_____

How far is too far for you?_____

_____

_____

_____

How does purity pave the way for intimacy? _____

_____

_____

_____

_____

God created sex. We don't know how the idea occurred to Him. But we do know that a long time ago in a galaxy far, far away, there was no sex. Then one day God said to Himself, probably out loud, "I've got a great idea!"

OK, so maybe my imagination is a little irreverent. But the fact remains, sex is a creation. It was and is God's idea. So it is safe to assume that He knows more about the subject than anyone—including Howard, Hugh, Dr. Ruth, and all of the assorted television and radio hosts who pollute the airways with their misinformation.

Sex can be unbelievably fulfilling (and fun). Or sex can leave a person feeling used and empty. Which do you suppose God intended? Sex is necessary for procreation, of course, but I think it is safe to assume that God wants our sexual experience to be fulfilling (and fun). So the next time you are praying alone or in your small group, go ahead and praise God out loud for the wonderful gift of sex. Don't hold back. Say something like, "This is the day that the Lord has made. And I'm grateful for sex too! God, You are cool!"

My point? God desires for us to experience sex in a way that fully exploits the joy and fulfillment of this wonderful

89

> God desires for us to experience sex in a way that fully exploits the joy and fulfillment of this wonderful gift—and that's within a marriage relationship.

gift—and that's within a marriage relationship. He wants our sexual experience to be the best it can possibly be. God has created you with the potential to experience great sex. Yea, God!

Today spend a significant amount of time mapping out your plan for remaining pure. Establish your moral boundaries. Write them down. Live by them. Start right now to pave the way for intimacy. Record your thoughts in the spaces below.

_____

_____

_____

_____

_____

_____

_____

_____

_____

_____

_____

_____

_____

_____

_____

_____

_____

_____

_____

Checkpoint #4

Healthy Friendships
Choosing Friends for Life

Principle
Your friends will determine the direction and quality of your life.

Critical Question
Are you establishing healthy friendships and avoiding unhealthy ones?

Key Passage
Proverbs 13:20

He who walks with the wise grows wise, but a companion of fools suffers harm.

Healthy Friendships
DILEMMA

For all of us who knew Josh Ming, Saturday, April 9, 1994, will always stand as a cruel reminder of the importance of healthy friendships. Josh was driving his cousin and two female passengers to a house in Shreveport, Louisiana, when four teenagers standing in the street began firing on the car. Josh was shot in the back of the head and killed in what police described as a "hail of gunfire." An estimated fifty-plus bullets hit the car.

The four teenagers arrested in the fatal shooting were known members of a gang of middle- and upper-class teens called The Fighting Irish. Josh's cousin was suspected of being involved in gang activity, as were the two girls in the car.

Josh was just giving his cousin a ride.

Josh was not a fool. He had given his life to Christ, and the change had been evident. Josh participated regularly at our weekly outreach event. He helped teach the children's choir at the church with his girlfriend, Jennifer. He was a member of the Airline High School football team. His grades were improving. Life was good.

On this one night, however, he was the companion of fools, and he suffered harm.

As a student it is imperative that you ask yourself this critical question: Am I establishing healthy friendships and avoiding unhealthy ones? Your answer will play a major role in how you conduct yourself throughout middle school and high school. It will help decide where you end up in your life's journey. Why? Because the friends you choose determine the direction and quality of your life. Let's talk about it.

Read Proverbs 13:20

According to this verse, what is the result of having a relationship with a wise person? _____

_____

_____

_____

_____

What is the result of having a relationship with a fool? _____

_____

_____

_____

_____

_____

Who wrote Proverbs? Do you think the identity of the writer gives validity to this principle? _____

_____

_____

_____

_____

Think about It

Write down the names of your closest friends._____

_____

_____

_____

Day One
Pursuing Wisdom

93

Which of your friends are wise? Are any of your friends fools? _____

_____

_____

_____

_____

_____

Have you ever suffered harm because of a friend? _____

_____

_____

_____

_____

94

Your friendships determine the direction and quality of your life. This principle is supported by more than mere observation. The Bible teaches it. Solomon, the wisest person who ever lived, illuminates this truth in Proverbs 13:20.

This powerful verse offers both a promise and a warning. The promise is that if you walk with wise friends, then you in turn will grow wise. The warning is that if you associate with fools, you will suffer harm.

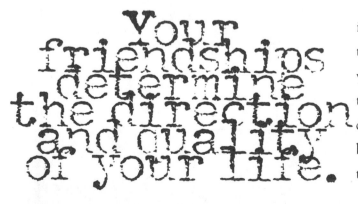

Let's look more closely at the promise. If you spend the majority of your time with wise people, Solomon says, you will become wise. In other words, the "wise" will rub off on you. But what does that mean? What does it mean to be wise? And is it really all that important to be wise? If you don't understand the benefits of being wise, this verse doesn't provide much motivation. But if you have a thirst in your heart for wisdom, then this verse has the potential to reformulate your thinking about friends.

There are three types of people mentioned in the book of Proverbs: the wise, the fool, and the scoffer. (Two are mentioned in Proverbs 13:20.) Find a Bible concordance and look up every verse in Proverbs that mentions these characters. Make a list of the terms and phrases that describe each one. Which one would you rather be? I think you'll agree it's much better to be wise!

The pursuit of wisdom will do more over the long haul to motivate you to rethink your friendships than anything else you can do. Develop a hunger in your heart for wisdom, and you will have the one tool you need to build healthy friendships—friendships that will benefit you now and for the rest of your life.

List below the ways the friends in your life determine the quality and direction of your life. Ask God to give you wisdom in the days ahead as we discover the truth about friends. Record what you ask for. _____

95

_____

_____

_____

_____

_____

_____

_____

_____

_____

_____

Day Two
The Right People

96

Read Proverbs 4:7

How much value does the writer put on wisdom? _____

_____

_____

_____

_____

_____

To what extreme does the writer challenge us to go to get wisdom? _____

_____

_____

_____

_____

Why do you think wisdom is so valuable? _____

_____

_____

_____

_____

_____

Think about It

Do you hunger for wisdom? Why or why not? _____

_____

_____

_____

How would you go about finding a wise friend? _____

_____

_____

_____

_____

Are you willing to pay a high price for a wise friend? Why or why not? _____

_____

_____

_____

_____

A wise person is someone who knows the difference between right and wrong and chooses to do what's right—even when it's hard. Unwise friends are pretty easy to spot. Wise ones are generally harder to find.

97

In fact, you may be quick to object to this whole principle about healthy friendships because you think you don't know any "wise" students. If wisdom is the primary criteria for friendship, you may feel as if you are facing the prospect of having no friends at all!

Wise friends are somewhat like owls. They are out there. They're just hard to spot. Why? For one thing, owls are quiet. They are still. They tend to blend in with the environment without making a scene. The few times I have seen owls in their natural habitat, someone has had to point them out to me. When they do make noise, the sound is unmistakable. But more times than not, finding an owl requires patient observation and a process of elimination. (*No, that's not an owl. Not that one either. That's not it. Not in that tree or that one….*)

Sometimes finding a wise friend can be a similar process. He or she may be difficult to spot at first. But by observing from a safe distance and noting the students who tend to make poor choices and suffer the consequences, you will be able to narrow the choices for a healthy friendship.

Several years ago a particular beer commercial sported the motto "Good times are made for good friends…it doesn't get any better than this." A scene slowly evolved of a group of friends sitting around a lakeside campfire, eating fresh fish, and drinking beer. The implication was that beer created good times that only could be experienced with good friends.

But good friends are wise friends. Good friends know the difference between right and wrong. Good friends make good decisions. And it will always be easier for you to do the right thing when you are with the right people.

Make a list of your close friends below. List the ways that you see them as wise or unwise. On paper, ask God to show you the truth about your friendships.

98

Friend	Wise	Unwise

Read Proverbs 14:8

According to this verse, what is "the wisdom of the prudent"? _____

_____

_____

_____

_____

_____

What is "the folly of fools"? _____

_____

Why does the writer describe these as opposite extremes? _____

_____

_____

_____

_____

Think about It

Do you have friends who tend to be deceptive in their relationships with their

parents, teachers, or peers? _____

_____

_____

_____

Define what you believe the writer means by a fool. _____

_____

_____

Day Three
Companion
of Fools

99

Could you be defined this way? _____

_____

_____

_____

_____

_____

A fool is someone who knows the difference between right and wrong but chooses to do what is wrong. Fools simply don't care about doing right. They are not ignorant—just uninterested. Pointing out the consequences of an action does not stop foolish people; they just do what they want to do when they want to do it. They feel that they are invincible. When it comes to using deception to serve their purposes, they don't hesitate. In fact, they are convinced they're superior to others when they successfully pull the wool over someone's eyes.

Proverbs 13:20 contains a wonderful promise, but it also contains a warning: "The companion of fools will suffer harm." In other words, if you spend the majority of your time with fools, there will be painful consequences.

Hanging around a fool doesn't mean you become a fool. It's worse than that. Something bad will eventually happen to you. When you associate with foolish friends, you unintentionally put yourself in harm's way. You make yourself a target. The verse doesn't say that harm *might* happen. It clearly states that the friend of fools *will* suffer harm.

> When you associate with foolish friends, you unintentionally put yourself in harm's way. You make yourself a target.

One of the recurring arguments students use with their parents and youth leaders goes something like this: "But I don't do what they do. I just want to be where they are." Or this: "I don't drink; I just go to the parties."

You need to stop and "give thought to [your] ways." Oftentimes it is not *what you do* that causes you to get hurt. It is *who you are with*. It is the *companion* of fools—not necessarily the fools themselves—who will suffer harm.

Have you ever been the companion of a fool and suffered harm? Ask God to give you discernment today on the friends in your life. Record what you pray.

_____

_____

_____

_____

_____

_____

_____

_____

_____

_____

_____

_____

_____

_____

_____

_____

101

Day Four
The Acceptance Magnet

102

Read Proverbs 13:10

What is the root cause of the quarrels that follow a fool? _____
_____
_____
_____

According to this verse, what is one way you can spot a person of wisdom? ____
_____
_____
_____
_____

Why do you think wisdom is so valuable? _____
_____
_____
_____
_____
_____
_____

Think about It

Are the friends you associate with always causing quarrels, chaos, and conflict?
_____
_____

Make of list of the top five qualities you want in a friend. Now list five qualities
you want in the people you date. _____
_____
_____

_____

_____

_____

_____

_____

Are your current friendships and dating relationships falling short of what you really want? _____

_____

_____

_____

_____

If you were to decide to choose a friend, what would the process look like? Would you interview candidates? Would you walk around with a list of desired characteristics, match them against the people you know, and yell "Bingo!" when you find someone who meets all the criteria? Think about it. What does it mean when we talk about "choosing friends"?

103

The truth is, you don't really choose your friends. You merely gravitate toward acceptance. You hook up with the people who are most accepting of you. Like all of us, you are an *acceptance magnet.*

Watch some friends walk into a party, and you will witness this principle in action. Those friends will naturally begin to communicate and interact with other peers that make them feel accepted. They will steer clear of the student or group of students that they sense dislikes or rejects them.

If this principle is true, you don't really choose your friends. *Your friends choose you.*

Acceptance is one of the strongest drives in life. Everybody wants to be liked, right? Students make decisions about their appearance and conduct based primarily on how it will affect their standing with those to whom they look for acceptance. They try to wring acceptance out of just about every environment in which they work, play, and live.

That is why some of your friends—maybe even you—can act so spiritual at youth group and live like the devil on the weekends. They want to fit in, and they are willing to adapt themselves to different environments in order to gain the acceptance they crave.

Bottom line, your choice of friends has more to do with your desire to be accepted than a list of characteristics you draw up. You don't *choose* your friends. You gravitate toward acceptance.

Make a list of your friends again. Did you choose them, or did they choose you? Do you struggle with acceptance? Be open and honest with God and tell Him why. _____

_____

_____

_____

_____

_____

_____

_____

_____

_____

104

Your choice of friends has more to do with your desire to be accepted than a list of characteristics you draw up.

Reread Proverbs 13:20

Do you think "walking with the wise" implies a deep friendship or simply an acquaintance relationship? _____

_____

_____

_____

_____

What does this verse say about the evolution of wisdom in your life?_____

_____

_____

_____

_____

How does growing wise connect with God's overall plan for your life? _____

_____

_____

_____

Think about It

When you think about your friendships, would you say that you chose your friends or your friends chose you? Why? _____

_____

_____

_____

_____

Day Five
Fleeing
Rejection

105

Checkpoint #4: Healthy Friendships

Do you have friends who have influence in your life simply because they have accepted you? _____

_____

_____

_____

Have you ever been rejected by a group of peers? Recount that story. _____

_____

_____

_____

_____

_____

_____

_____

_____

Acceptance is a good thing. There is nothing wrong with wanting to be accepted. But acceptance by the wrong people can be detrimental to your life. Why? Because *acceptance paves the way to influence*.

This is a principle you need to keep in sight at all times. Acceptance and influence are inexorably linked. Think about it: You resist the influence of those you feel don't accept you. When you feel accepted, however, you drop your guard. You let them in. You listen to them. There is no sustained influence apart from acceptance.

Acceptance is only one side of the coin. You and your friends are not only gravitating toward acceptance, you are fleeing rejection. Nothing hurts like rejection. We all go to extreme measures to avoid it.

Listen to how Stuart Hall, coauthor of *The Seven Checkpoints Student Journal*, recounts this story of rejection from his childhood:

Because of my family's financial status when I was growing up, I never had the coolest name-brand clothes. One year my parents bought me two pair of Sears Tuffskin jeans for school, a brown pair and a blue pair. All the cool kids had Levi's with the silver or red tabs. I had two pair of Tuffskins that had to last all year! When my jeans started wearing out and getting holes in them, my mom, who was big into cross-stitching, made a huge Indian head on the leg of my brown jeans and an American flag on the rear end of my blue jeans. I can still hear kids pledging allegiance to my rear end and calling me "Tonto." I vowed that I would never have to face that kind of rejection again.

Like Stuart, most teenagers have been laughed at or put down enough to know that they want to avoid rejection at any cost. Eric Harris, one of the two young gunmen in the 1999 Columbine High School tragedy, wrote in his academic day planner, "The lonely man strikes with absolute rage." Harris and his accomplice, Dylan Klebold, both wrote of not being accepted, of being rejected, of not fitting in. In an Associated Press article by Steven K. Paulson, we learned that investigators who analyzed their writings concluded, "They plotted against all those persons who found them offensive—jocks, girls who said no, other outcasts, or anybody they thought did not accept them."

Rejection and acceptance are powerful forces of human nature. We all have the propensity to do

107

Nothing hurts like rejection. We all go to extreme measures to avoid it.

whatever it takes to avoid the former and gain the latter. As a Christian, you need to find your acceptance based on your relationship with Christ. He is the ultimate friend!

Today record the ways you feel rejected. Ask God to heal your hurts and allow you to feel His unconditional love and acceptance. Write your thoughts down! _____

_____

_____

_____

_____

_____

_____

_____

_____

_____

_____

_____

_____

_____

_____

_____

_____

108

Read 1 Samuel 18:1

What do you think caused Jonathan to become "one in spirit" with David?
(Hint: Read 1 Samuel 17.) _____

_____

_____

_____

_____

_____

What do you think "one in spirit" means? _____

_____

_____

_____

Do you think David's life was appealing to Jonathan?_____

_____

_____

_____

_____

Think about It

Do you have a friend with whom you feel one in spirit? Explain. _____

_____

_____

_____

Day Six
Genuine Friends

109

How did you choose that friend? _____

_____

_____

_____

_____

_____

Can you honestly say that you love that friend as yourself? Why or why not?

_____

_____

_____

_____

_____

110

As you evaluate the genuineness of your friendships, you need to become sensitive to three factors:

1. The direction of the relationship

Relationships don't stand still. They are always moving in one direction or another. The tendency is to evaluate a friendship based on where it is at a particular point in time. You need to become sensitive to the direction of a relationship as well as to what is happening at any given moment.

Genuine friendships move in a positive, mutually beneficial direction. A counterfeit friend will move the relationship the other way. Ask, "If this relationship continues to move in the current direction, where will it eventually end up?" And secondly, "Is that where I want to be?"

Genuine friendships move in a positive, mutually beneficial direction.

2. Self-destructive behavior

Counterfeit friends will usually exhibit some form of self-destructive behavior. Perhaps they will seem incapable of making wise choices. They may tend to get in the same trouble over and over. Most likely they will scorn the authority figures in their lives.

The reason self-destructive behavior is important for you to look out for is that if your friends won't watch out for themselves, they certainly won't be looking out for *your* best interests. If someone doesn't take good care of his or her car, I will certainly think twice before I loan that person mine!

You are always at risk when you associate with self-destructive friends. If they aren't committed to taking care of themselves, they certainly won't take care of *you.*

> You are always at risk when you associate with self-destructive friends.

111

3. A lack of solid convictions

A person who lacks convictions will have a difficult time being a true friend. Listen for statements such as:

✔ **"You have to do what you feel is right for you."**

✔ **"Everybody has to decide for themselves."**

✔ **"No one can tell other people what is right for them."**

These are the mantras of those who have no solid convictions—who drift along with the emotion of the moment. You can be sure these "friends" won't stand with you when you must stand up for what is right in the sight of God but unpopular with many of them.

Friendships that fail these three tests are not genuine; they're counterfeit. You must move counterfeit friends out of your circle of influence and into your circle of concern. What that actually means will depend upon the circumstances surrounding the friendship. It may mean cutting yourself off completely from that person; it might mean keeping some distance and adding him or her to your prayer list. But bottom line, you must make some changes.

This is admittedly a painful process. One of the most difficult things you will ever be called upon to do is to walk away from destructive relationships with people you've come to care about. It is difficult, but it is necessary. After all, your friendships—especially those within your closest circle of influence—will determine the direction and quality of your life.

Using the factors of genuine friendship listed above, list your friends and record where you think your relationship is going based on these three factors. Ask God to give you courage to make hard choices as it relates to your friends. Write it down. _____

_____

_____

_____

_____

_____

_____

_____

_____

_____

_____

_____

112

You must move counterfeit friends out of your circle of influence and into your circle of concern.

Read 1 Samuel 18:3–4

What does Jonathan making a "covenant" with David mean to you?

_____

_____

_____

_____

In what way do you think the exchanging of robes was significant? _____

_____

_____

_____

How was the exchanging of weapons significant? _____

_____

_____

_____

_____

_____

Think about It

Think of your deepest friendship. How deep is that friendship? Is that friendship

rooted in Christ? _____

_____

_____

_____

_____

_____

Day Seven
Circles of
Friendship

113

Read Colossians 3:10. How does this verse parallel the exchanging of robes in 1 Samuel 18:4? _____

_____

_____

_____

_____

Do your friends strengthen you in the places where you are weak? _____

_____

_____

_____

_____

_____

114

"The issue is not whether or not your friends are good people. It is whether or not your friendships are healthy and going in the right direction."

What do you do once you realize that the people you thought were your true friends are really counterfeit friends? To help answer that question, consider this diagram of the concentric circles of friendship:

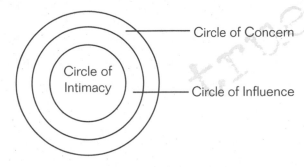

Please don't think I don't care about your friends or don't want you to have relationships with peers who still need Christ. The issue is not whether or not your friends are "good people." It is whether or not your friendships are healthy and going in the right direction.

The concentric circles can help you keep this sensitive subject in proper perspective. All of your friends fall into one of three categories. The outer circle represents the friends you are concerned about. These may be your non-Christian friends or Christian friends who are going through a tough time—anyone you consider a friend and for whom you feel a sense of concern. These are peers you hope to influence.

The second circle, the circle of influence, represents the friends you allow to influence you. You know who they are. You know who the positive and negative influences are in your life. It is in this circle that you must identify those friends who are not genuine. You don't have to abandon them completely; you simply need to move them further out, into your circle of concern. Perhaps one day you will be able to move them back again into a place of influence in your life.

115

The third circle, the circle of intimacy, is reserved for one person: the man or woman you will meet someday, fall in love with, and marry. With this in mind, you need to choose the people you date from your circle of influence, not your circle of concern.

Today think of all of the friends you know and determine which circle they belong to. Make changes if necessary, particularly in your circle of influence. Remember, your friends help determine the direction and quality of your life. Record your thoughts. _____

_____

_____

_____

_____

_____

_____

_____

_____

_____

_____

_____

_____

_____

_____

_____

Checkpoint #5

Wise Choices
Walking Wisely
in a Fool's World

Principle

Walk wisely.

Critical Question

Are you making wise choices in every area of your life?

Key Passage

Ephesians 5:15–17

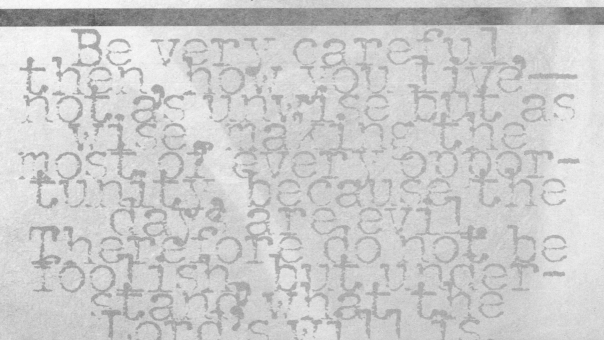

Be very careful,
then, how you live—
not as unwise but as
wise, making the
most of every oppor-
tunity, because the
days are evil.
Therefore do not be
foolish, but under-
stand what the
Lord's will is.

Wise Choices
DILEMMA

Every Friday night after the football game, Sam and his ninth-grade buddies like to drop in at the local pizza place. Their habit is to make sure they snag the booth right behind the one occupied by one of his friend's big brother. Big brother orders a pitcher of beer, pours a couple of glasses, and passes them back to Sam and his underage friends.

Sam described to me the battle he fights every Friday night as he sits there and tries not to sip the beer. "Sometimes I can make it through the whole night," he said. "But most of the time, I join in with everybody else." He swore up and down that he never got drunk. But he knew he had no business drinking.

What would you do if you were in his shoes? What do you think Sam should do?

Unfortunately for Sam, when he asked for my advice I was all too ready with an answer. "Quit going to get pizza with your friends after the football game," I told him. And as I expected, he looked at me like I was crazy.

"But what's wrong with getting pizza with my friends?" he asked.

"Nothing," I said. "But that's not really the issue. The issue is, in light of your past experience—knowing that you will be tempted to drink when you go out for pizza—what is the wise thing to do?"

Sam shrugged his shoulders, said he would think about it, and walked away.

Whenever you are faced with an opportunity, an invitation, or a desire, you will eventually pose the question, Is there anything wrong with this? Your assumption is that if something is not wrong, then it must be right. If you have never heard a sermon against it, don't know any Bible verses condemning it, or see that other Christians are involved, your natural tendency is to conclude that it must be OK.

But the question you are really asking is this: How close can I get to sin without actually sinning?

The truth is, you are always just one decision away from helping or hurting your life and relationships. Are your making wise choices? Let's talk about it.

relationships

wise choices

Day One
The Wise Thing to Do

Read Ephesians 5:15–17

Why do you think Paul encourages us to be "very careful" about how we live? _____

_____

_____

_____

What is his solution for living a careful life? _____

_____

_____

_____

_____

Is this a suggestion or a command? _____

_____

_____

_____

_____

_____

Think about It

Would you say that you live a careful life? Why or why not? _____

_____

_____

_____

_____

120

Do you have defined boundaries in these areas: music, alcohol, drugs, sex? What are those boundaries? _____

_____

_____

_____

_____

_____

Does wisdom play a part in your decision-making process when it comes to these areas?_____

_____

_____

_____

_____

_____

121

How close can I get to sin without actually sinning? I'm quite sure you have asked that question in some form when other questions have come up in your daily life—questions like:

- ✔ **What type of music can I listen to?**

- ✔ **Can I date non-Christians?**

- ✔ **How far is too far?**

- ✔ **Can I attend parties?**

- ✔ **Is it all right for me to have a beer?**

- ✔ **Which movies are OK for me to see?**

Checkpoint #5: Wise Choices

Instead of evaluating opportunities, invitations, and desires by the standard of "Is anything wrong with this?" you need to ask a new question—a question that takes you to the heart of the issues that you struggle with daily. You need to ask, "Is this the *wise* thing for me to do?"

The apostle Paul encouraged the believers in Ephesus to examine all of life through the lens of wisdom. He instructed them to be careful to walk out their lives "not as unwise men, but as wise, making the most of your time, because the days are evil."

That's good advice. In order to help the students in my youth group make wise decisions, I developed a little rhyme that summarizes this principle in a way that's easy to remember. As you make decisions each day, perhaps you can remember it too:

> **There's good and there's bad...**
> **But that is not our cue.**
> **But rather...**
> **What is the wise thing to do?**

What is your response to that? Record your thoughts in the spaces below.

_____

_____

_____

_____

_____

_____

_____

Reread Ephesians 5:15–17

What does Paul mean by "opportunity" in verse 16? _____

_____

_____

_____

_____

Define "evil" in your own words. _____

_____

_____

_____

What does Paul encourage as our response to evil days? _____

_____

_____

_____

_____

Think about It

If the most poisonous snake in the world were crawling under your feet right now, what would you do? _____

_____

Why would you do that? _____

_____

_____

_____

_____

Day Two

Anticipating Trouble

123

Can you name one choice you made that totally changed the direction of your life? Explain that choice. _____

_____

_____

_____

_____

God wants you to learn how to anticipate trouble, not walk blindly into it. Whether you realize it or not, you live in a dangerous world—one that is designed to destroy your mind, your body, your relationships, and your self-esteem. That is why Paul says "the days are evil." They were evil then, and they are evil now.

The Bible advises you to be very careful as you approach your world. That term *careful* carries with it the idea of scoping out a situation. Clearly God wants you to anticipate things that are harmful before it is too late to avoid them.

In dangerous environments people take extraordinary precautions. Think of all the equipment a fireman puts on before rushing into a burning building. Or think of all the checks, double checks, and triple checks NASA goes through before sending a manned shuttle into space. The environment demands such meticulous measures. That's why Paul goes on to say, "Therefore do not be foolish...." In other words, you must never lose sight of the nature of what is going on around you. You can't approach life blindly, as if all is well.

You may have a hard time believing that you are always just one decision away from doing irreversible damage to your life and relationships, but it is true. Time and maturity

124

God wants you to learn how to anticipate trouble, not walk blindly into it.

will make that truth more apparent. Along the way you will gain scars that won't allow you to forget.

Let's face it: Students tend to think they are invincible. In that naiveté they are prone to approach the world as if it is a safe place to be. You need to begin to paint a realistic picture of what is lurking out there in the "real world." It is imperative that you equip yourself with the necessary tools to steer clear of those relationships and opportunities that have the potential to hurt you.

Wisdom is one of God's primary navigational tools for life. If you can learn to run everything that comes your way through the grid of "Is this the wise thing to do?" you will have taken a big step toward preparing yourself for these evil days.

Do you consider yourself wise? Ask God to help you gain perspective! Write down your prayer. _____

_____

_____

_____

_____

_____

_____

_____

_____

_____

125

Day Three

Facing the Truth

126

Reread Ephesians 5:15–17

What does Paul want us to do instead of being foolish? _____

_____

_____

_____

How can you understand God's will? _____

_____

_____

_____

Why do you think Paul wants us to understand God's will? _____

_____

_____

_____

_____

_____

Think about It

In your own words, explain what Paul is encouraging you to do in this passage.

_____

_____

_____

_____

_____

How does knowing God's will relate to making wise decisions? _____

_____

_____

_____

_____

Is there an area of your life in which you are not being honest with yourself—where you know deep down what the Lord's will is, but you're not doing it? _____

_____

_____

_____

_____

_____

_____

_____

If a certain group of friends gets you in trouble over and over, somehow you have got to find the courage and humility to admit it.

The apostle Paul follows his admonition to be careful with a fascinating charge: "Understand what the Lord's will is." This statement was puzzling to me at first. How can Paul command us to *understand* something? After all, if you don't understand something, being told to understand does nothing to lift you beyond your confusion.

But what Paul means is this: *Face up to what you know in your heart is the will of the Lord.* In learning to make wise decisions, a critical part of this process is being willing and committed to face up to what you know in your heart is true. As long as you aren't being honest with yourself, wisdom will elude you.

Being honest with others is difficult enough, but being honest with yourself is sometimes more painful. You may figure that as long as others (your parents, your

Be honest with yourself— and begin to walk wisely.

teachers, your strong Christian friends) don't know what you're doing, you're not really hurting yourself. All the while, those friends who continually drag you down, those movies that cause you to struggle in your thought life, or those Friday nights of binge drinking strangle the life from your soul and draw you away from the life of wisdom that God wants you to live.

Be honest! If a certain group of friends gets you in trouble over and over, somehow you have got to find the courage and humility to admit it. As we have seen already, your friends will help determine the quality and direction of your life. If certain forms of entertainment cause you to sin, you must be honest with yourself. The fact that something is funny or thrilling does not mean that it is wise. If certain songs send your mind in a direction it shouldn't go, face it. It just isn't wise to keep listening!

Once you are willing to face up to the truth that is rattling around in your heart, the wise thing to do will become apparent in every situation. Be honest with yourself—and begin to walk wisely.

Be honest on paper. Record those places where you are being foolish. Write down what you think needs to be your course of action. Ask God for wisdom.

_____

_____

_____

_____

_____

_____

Day Four
Planning Not To

Read Proverbs 28:26

What is the promise in this scripture for those who walk wisely? _____

_____

_____

What does the writer mean by "kept safe"? _____

_____

_____

_____

_____

What does a fool trust in? _____

_____

_____

_____

_____

129

Think about It

Think of one mistake you have made that continues to haunt you to this day.

How and why did you make it? _____

_____

_____

_____

_____

_____

What have been the consequences of that mistake? _____

_____

_____

_____

_____

Has God ever delivered you from something? How did He deliver you? _____

_____

_____

_____

_____

_____

_____

130

According to the writer of Proverbs, God promises to protect you if you walk wisely. He promises to keep you safe. But safe from what? Think about the mistakes you have made up to this point in your life. What would you have been kept safe from if you had made wise choices? Guilt? Memories? A bad reputation? Impurity? Scars?

Let's face it. Most students don't stay up late at night planning to get into trouble. Sin and its consequences always surprise you. Nothing, it seems, is ever intentional on your part. Have you ever made any of these statements?

✔ **"I don't know how it happened."**

✔ **"I didn't know he would_____."**

- ✔ "I didn't know it was spiked."

- ✔ "I didn't plan to_____."

- ✔ "It was the first time."

The problem is not that most students plan to get into trouble. The problem is that most students don't plan *not to*. I have never met a student who planned to:

- ✔ drift away from the Lord

- ✔ get pregnant

- ✔ become addicted to alcohol or tobacco

- ✔ become alienated from his or her mom and dad

- ✔ get arrested

- ✔ ruin his or her reputation

But I have met hundreds of students who never planned *not to*. Wisdom is God's tool to protect you from the things that have the potential to destroy your life. To walk wisely, you need to be proactive. You need to plan *not to*.

In what areas of your life do you need to be proactive? Write them down in detail. _____

_____

_____

_____

The problem is not that most students plan to get into trouble. The problem is that most students don't plan131 not to.

Day Five
The Compass of Experience

132

Read Proverbs 3:13–18

What do you think the writer means when he says that the man who finds wisdom is "blessed"? _____

_____

_____

_____

Make a list of the attributes of wisdom listed in this passage. _____

_____

_____

_____

_____

_____

How does wisdom "yield better returns than gold"? _____

_____

_____

_____

_____

Think about It

How do you gain wisdom? _____

_____

_____

_____

_____

Someone has defined wisdom as "the sum of knowledge plus action." What does that definition mean to you? _____

_____

_____

_____

_____

How do you determine what is wise and what is not wise? _____

_____

_____

_____

_____

_____

_____

133

As you navigate the journey of life, it is important for you to develop an internal "compass" to help you stay on course. The question, Is this the wise thing to do? must become so ingrained in your heart and mind that it becomes a natural reaction when you are presented with a choice.

The past is one thing that can serve as a compass for the present. A wise student will learn to evaluate opportunities, invitations, and relationships based upon his or her past experiences. Someone once said that example and experience are the greatest schools of humanity. Your past experiences are not just fodder for guilt or memories. If you are committed to walking

The past is one thing that can serve as a compass for the present.

wisely, then you must learn how to use the compass of past experience to guide you now and into the future.

Remember Sam, the ninth grader I told you about in the opening to this section? He liked to go to the local pizza joint with his buddies on Friday nights. And every Friday night, he found himself tempted to drink beer with his friends. Often he gave in.

Sam knew he shouldn't be drinking. But when he asked me, "What do you think I should do?" he wasn't happy with my answer.

"Quit going to get pizza with your friends after the football game," I told him.

"But what's wrong with getting pizza with my friends?" he asked.

Of course, there is nothing inherently wrong with going out for pizza with a group of friends. For another student, drinking might not be a temptation in that situation. For Sam, however, it was. Sam needed to ask himself, "In light of *my* past experience, what is the wise thing for *me* to do?"

You must understand that *your* past experience dictates what is and isn't wise for *you*. The compass of past experience is going to work its way out in your life in unique and specific ways. What is wise for one person is not always wise for another. Follow your compass!

In light of your past experiences, record the things you know you should avoid to be wise. What do you have to do to avoid these situations or people?

_____

_____

_____

_____

_____

_____

Read Psalm 111:10

Day Six

The Compass of
Current Events

What does this verse say is the beginning of wisdom? _____

_____

_____

_____

What do you think the writer means by the "fear of the Lord"? _____

_____

_____

_____

_____

Why is it significant that the psalmist talks about the *beginning* of wisdom?

135

_____

_____

_____

_____

Think about It

Do you agree with this statement: "What is wise for you today is not necessarily wise for you tomorrow"? Explain. _____

_____

_____

_____

_____

_____

At what times and in what circumstances are you the most vulnerable to sin and temptation? _____

_____

_____

_____

_____

Ask, "In light of what's happening around me right now, what is the wise thing to do?"

How can wisdom help you when you are vulnerable?

_____

_____

_____

_____

_____

_____

136

Current events are also a factor in determining what is and isn't wise—another compass to help you walk wisely through life. You need to learn to ask, "In light of what's happening around me right now, what is the wise thing to do?" After all, we are all more vulnerable at certain times than at others. What is wise today may not be wise tomorrow.

Students tend to be particularly vulnerable to temptation:

- ✔ **right after an argument with their parents**

- ✔ **right after final exams**

- ✔ **during spring break**

- ✔ **right after a breakup**

✔ during family conflict

✔ when they enter a new school

These times of stress or transition call for a heightened commitment to doing the wise thing. There is a direct relationship between these kinds of circumstances and your own vulnerability. Again, you must learn to ask, "In light of what's happening around me *right now,* what is the wise thing to do?"

Several years ago I drove a van loaded with students to summer camp. Two eleventh-grade girls sat directly behind me. They were lost in conversation, totally unaware that I could hear everything they were saying.

Eventually their conversation turned to boys. Then boyfriends. Then how far each was willing to go with their boyfriends. (They were fairly explicit.)

I knew their conversation wasn't really any of my business. But like a good pastor I turned down the radio, pushed back in my seat, and listened in. Here's how the conversation ended—minus the unnecessary details:

First girl: "Would you let Jeremy _____?"

Long pause.

Second girl: "Well, if I just had a fight with my mom, I might."

I almost drove off the road. Everything in me wanted to turn around in my seat and say, "What does having a fight with your mom have to do with it?" But I didn't. And after I had thought about it for a while, I realized that I had seen this kind of twisted reasoning play itself out in other situations. Students often attempt to "get back" at their parents by doing something self-destructive. It doesn't make any sense, but that's how their minds work.

You are definitely more vulnerable at some times than at others. That is why

137

you must learn to ask the wisdom question within the context of your immediate surroundings and emotional state. Ask:

- ✔ **In light of what I have just been through, what is the wise thing to do?**

- ✔ **In light of what is going on at home, what is the wise thing to do?**

- ✔ **In light of what's happening at school or with my studies, what is the wise thing to do?**

- ✔ **In light of how I'm feeling, what is the wise thing to do?**

If you learn to use the compass of current events (along with the compass of past experience) to make your decisions each day, you will be well on the road to walking wisely through life.

List the times in your life when you think you are the most vulnerable. Ask God on paper to help you stay wise when it is hard not to be a fool. _____

_____

_____

_____

_____

_____

_____

_____

_____

_____

_____

_____

138

You are definitely more vulnerable at some times than at others.

Read Proverbs 1:7 and 12:1

Day Seven
Fools and Scoffers

What does a fool despise? _____

_____

_____

_____

Why do you think loving discipline is like loving wisdom? _____

_____

_____

_____

_____

Why is it stupid to hate correction? _____

139

_____

_____

_____

_____

_____

_____

Think about It

Define a fool in your own words. _____

_____

_____

_____

_____

_____

Can you think of someone who you would consider a fool? Explain. _____

_____

_____

_____

_____

_____

Think about your own reaction to discipline and correction. For the most part, would you say that you have been wise or foolish? _____

_____

_____

_____

_____

140

There are options when it comes to how we walk in life. You need to understand that if you decide not to embrace wisdom as a guiding principle, you are opting for something else by default. You never walk away from something without walking toward something else.

The Book of Proverbs describes three kinds of people: the wise, the fools, and the scoffers. We've talked a great deal about what it means to be wise. Let's look more closely now at the other two categories.

You never walk away from something without walking toward something else.

Fools are those people who know right from wrong and choose to do what is wrong. They could care less about doing what is right. Fools are not guided by a predetermined standard of behavior but follow their immediate desires. They do what they feel like doing. They go with the emotional flow. Fools generally don't have reasons to explain their behavior; they just do what they want to do regardless of the consequences.

Fools will not take instruction because they believe they already know everything. The Bible gives us a vivid word picture of how a fool receives counsel in Proverbs 26:7: "Like a lame man's legs that hang limp is a proverb [wisdom] in the mouth of a fool."

Scoffers, like fools, are those who know right from wrong and choose to do what is wrong. But scoffers go a step further. They criticize the wise. Scoffers are those students who present themselves as too cool for everyone else in the youth group. They refuse to worship. They refuse to participate in Bible study. What's worse, they look for opportunities to make fun of the students who do these things. They are arrogant, smart-mouthed, and condescending. They consistently ridicule those students who are trying to do what's right.

Unfortunately for them, scoffers tend to make very unwise decisions over time. Their decisions often lead them into a downward spiral that culminates in tragedy and destruction. When scoffers need wisdom most, it is nowhere to be found. In their attempt to distance themselves from wise people, they distance themselves from wisdom—and that ultimately comes back to haunt them.

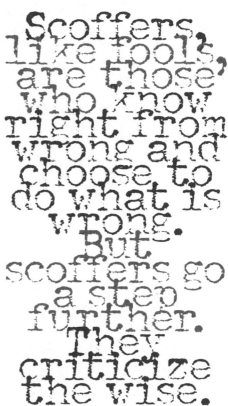

Scoffers, like fools, are those who know right from wrong and choose to do what is wrong. But scoffers go a step further. They criticize the wise.

Every student I have ever visited in an alcohol or drug rehabilitation program, every pregnant teenager I have ever met, and every young inmate I have ever spoken to in depth has in some form or fashion admitted to making "stupid" decisions. And every one of them thought they were too smart, too cool, or too careful to get burned. Such is the story of the scoffer.

Remember, you are always one decision away from helping or hurting your life and relationships. Don't be a fool or a scoffer. Choose to be wise.

Do you have fools or scoffers in your circle of friends? Pray for them today. Ask God to move in their lives. _____

_____

_____

_____

_____

_____

_____

_____

142

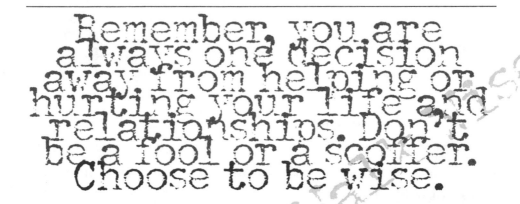

Remember, you are always one decision away from helping or hurting your life and relationships. Don't be a fool or a scoffer. Choose to be wise.

Checkpoint #6
Ultimate Authority
Finding Freedom under God

Principle
Maximum freedom is found under God's authority.

Critical Question
Are you submitting to the authorities God has placed over you?

Key Passage
Romans 13:1–2

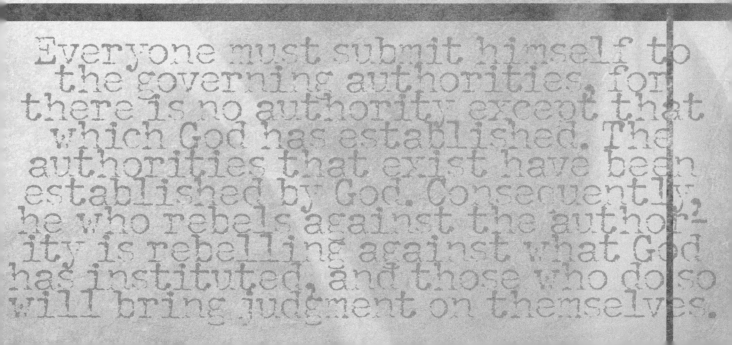

Everyone must submit himself to the governing authorities, for there is no authority except that which God has established. The authorities that exist have been established by God. Consequently, he who rebels against the authority is rebelling against what God has instituted, and those who do so will bring judgment on themselves.

Ultimate Authority
DILEMMA

Rodney was not the kind of kid most people would immediately be drawn to. In fact, they generally tended to shy away from him. His appearance probably had something to do with it. He always wore his black trench coat and "Indiana Jones" hat, even in the heat of summer. His demeanor shouted of aloofness and a general disregard for mankind.

What really set Rodney apart from others, however, was the fact that he never seemed to smile. The few times I got close enough to Rodney to have intelligent conversation, I walked away with the haunting realization that this young man was *not* a happy camper. His beady eyes seemed to stare a hole right through me, and the blank, expressionless look on his face always left me uneasy. It didn't help to know that he was fixated on hard-core rock music and the philosophies of Marilyn Manson.

Rodney was unreachable, I thought. No doubt we would hear about him one day on the police blotter.

Rodney's sister, however, was a very committed believer who loved God passionately. She was very concerned about her brother. One night, because of his sister's love and persistence, Rodney decided to give this "church deal" a chance. God spoke to him deeply. I will never forget sitting down with Rodney afterward. With tears streaming down his face, he could barely explain what was going on inside of him. What came out was his story.

I had known that Rodney's mom and dad were divorced, but I didn't know why. It turned out that Rodney's father was in prison. Rodney had idolized his dad and put his trust in him, only to be crushed by his arrest. What poured out of

Rodney that night was the anger, frustration, resentment, and distrust that had built up over a period of time. It had shaped Rodney's personality. It had forged his moral structure. It had stolen any peace and joy he had ever had.

Because Rodney looked on his father now with anger and disgust, he gave no other authority in his life any respect or leverage. In fact, he did exactly the opposite. He rebelled against his mom. He rebelled against society. He rebelled against God. Anyone considered an authority by the world's standards was an enemy to Rodney—including me.

Rodney's story is not unlike the stories of countless peers you interact with every day. Whether they are extremists like Rodney or simply normal students having trouble obeying their parents, most teenagers struggle with the issue of authority. The underlying issue for Rodney was his loss of respect and faith in his father as a godly authority in his life. The greater issue, however, was his unwillingness to recognize and submit to God's control over all authority.

The truth is, maximum freedom in life is found only under God's authority. Do you find it hard to submit to the authorities God has placed over your life? Let's talk about it.

145

Day One
Absolute Freedom

146

Read Genesis 3:1–24

What was Satan trying to do by asking the question in verse 1? _____

_____

_____

_____

Whose integrity was he calling into doubt when he stated, "You will not surely

die"? _____

_____

_____

_____

What was the difference between what God had said to Adam and Eve and

what Satan was now telling them? _____

_____

_____

_____

_____

Think about It

Why were Adam and Eve the freest people who have ever lived? _____

_____

_____

_____

How did Satan convince them to break God's one rule? _____

_____

_____

_____

_____

What was the immediate result of Adam and Eve's breaking the rule? What was
the long-term result? _____

_____

_____

_____

_____

Adam and Eve were the freest people who have ever walked the face of this
planet. Why? They lived in a "one-rule" world. They were given only one "Thou
shalt not." God said they could do whatever they wanted to *except* eat from the
tree of the knowledge of good and evil. Tend the garden. Name the animals.
Multiply. Just don't touch that tree.

I love to talk to students about the world of Adam and Eve. Like most
teenagers, I grew up thinking that God loved rules. I assumed that He got a kick
out of saying no. But in His ideal world—a world that was just the way He wanted
it—He only instituted one rule. Why? Because *God is not into rules*. God loves
and values freedom.

Adam and Eve were happy in God's one-rule world until Satan came along
and convinced them that they were not absolutely free. The implication of his
devious line of questioning in Genesis 3 was that God was holding out on them,
that there was a level of freedom they were missing out on. Ultimately, in an
attempt to reach for absolute freedom, they chose the way of disobedience and
rebellion to God's authority. The premise of their decision was that *rebellion*
brings freedom.

Rebellion was and is the attitude and act of disobeying God's rule. Adam and

147

Eve were convinced that freedom could be found in doing what was forbidden. What they soon realized was that they *lost* their freedom because of their rebellion. No longer would they live in the garden. They would work hard for their food. They would experience pain in childbearing.

Interestingly enough, our society is full of rules today because of Adam and Eve's unwillingness to submit to God's authority. They broke one rule. Now we are inundated with rules.

Sound like freedom to you?

There is a significant principle behind God's command to Adam and Eve: *Maximum freedom is found under God's authority.* That seems so counterintuitive to most of us. How can you be under authority *and* be free? How can you follow a standard of rules yet have the freedom to choose what you want to do? Isn't that a contradiction?

Not at all! Life bears out the truth of this principle. Maximum freedom is found under God's authority—and only under God's authority. Unfortunately, Adam and Eve learned this truth a little too late. It's not too late for you.

What do you think about this issue? Record your initial thoughts in the spaces below. _____

_____

_____

_____

_____

_____

_____

_____

148

Maximum freedom is found under God's authority—and only under God's authority.

Read Romans 13:1–2 and 1 Peter 2:13–15

What is the foundational principle on authority found in Romans 13:1?_____

_____

_____

_____

According to Romans 13:2, what are people really doing when they rebel

against authority? _____

_____

_____

_____

_____

What is the reason given in 1 Peter 2:13–15 for submitting to authority? _____

_____

_____

_____

Think about It

List all the authorities you have in your life (parents, coaches, teachers, etc.).

_____

_____

_____

_____

Put a check by the authorities on your list that you have rebelled against at one

time or another.

Have you ever thought about the fact that when you rebelled against each of

149

these authorities, you were ultimately rebelling against God? _____

_____

_____

Maximum freedom is found under God's authority because *God ultimately establishes every authority*. Paul, in his letter to the church in Rome, makes this clear. If God is ultimately behind all authority, then authority issues are ultimately spiritual issues. You cannot pursue intimacy with God and ignore your conflicts with authority. Or to say it another way, you cannot be right with God and out of sorts with the authorities God has placed over you.

Can freedom and authority coexist? Most teenagers believe freedom is a world without authority. That is a lie that may rob you of your freedom. Let me illustrate.

Bobby's parents have set some boundaries that they expect Bobby to respect. Nothing unrealistic or dogmatic—just some standards to live by. Their intention is to keep Bobby out of harm's way and to protect his best interests.

One of those boundaries is that Bobby will not drink nor hang around anyone who has been drinking alcohol, regardless of how good a friend that person may be. Bobby loves his parents and understands what they are trying to do. But he sees their efforts to protect him as overbearing and stifling. None of his friends' parents enforce the same rule, and he feels he is old enough to be responsible when it comes to drinking.

Bobby decides to disobey his parents' wishes one night and goes out to party with his friends. He doesn't drink much, but his friends do. On their way home, with a drunken friend at the wheel, their car swerves into the path of a family in a van. The wreck is horrific. The mother and three kids in the van are all killed instantly. Bobby's friend, the driver, dies as well.

150

God ultimately establishes every authority.

Let's think about what Bobby's desire for freedom has granted him:

- ✔ He has lost a friend.

- ✔ He has had a part in the death of a woman and three kids.

- ✔ He has seen families devastated for years to come.

- ✔ He has broken the law by drinking while under the legal age.

- ✔ He will probably spend some time incarcerated.

- ✔ He may lose his driving privileges.

- ✔ He will lose the trust of his parents.

- ✔ He will lose the trust of his peers.

- ✔ He will probably lose friends.

The list could go on and on. Sound like freedom to you?

The point is that God wants us to be as free as we can be. But maximum freedom is found *under authority*. Breaking the rules or having no rules at all will not bring freedom. Jesus once said that truth sets us free. God is truth, and it is under His authority that we gain true freedom.

Personalize this story. Record a time in your life when you rebelled against authority. How did you lose freedom? Write it down. _____

_____

_____

_____

_____

_____

_____

You cannot pursue intimacy with God and ignore your conflicts with authority.

151

Day Three
Under Authority

152

Read Matthew 8:5–10

What is the principle on authority the Roman centurion was referring to in his discussion with Jesus? _____

_____

_____

_____

How were the centurion and Jesus similar as it relates to authority? _____

_____

_____

_____

What was the centurion doing by asking Jesus for help? _____

_____

_____

_____

_____

Think about It

Is it difficult for you to stay under authority? Explain. _____

_____

_____

_____

_____

_____

_____

Do you fear authority? Why or why not? _____
_____
_____
_____

What is the relationship between what God may ultimately want to do through you and the authorities He places over you?_____
_____
_____
_____
_____

To have authority, you must be under authority.

153

The Gospels tell us repeatedly about people being in awe of Jesus because of His authority to heal the sick, restore life to the dead, calm storms, and command demons to flee. But how did Jesus view His own authority? His interaction with the Roman centurion in Matthew 8 gives us an interesting perspective.

The Bible says that Jesus was "astonished" at the centurion's understanding of the principle of authority. Apparently this Roman soldier recognized something that many of Christ's closest followers failed to grasp: *Jesus Himself was under authority.* When the centurion gave orders to men below him in rank, those men obeyed because they knew he was operating under the authority of the Roman state. He had authority because he was under authority. As he watched Jesus exercise authority over disease and demons, it occurred to him that Christ must be under some divine authority to be able to wield that kind of power.

This short encounter illustrates an important principle: *To have authority, you must be under authority.* The authority that Jesus had to do His amazing miracles was granted to Him by God. Jesus was under His Father's authority. Consequently, He had authority.

There is a direct relationship between what God ultimately wants to do through you and the authorities He places over you. Are you under authority?

Record the places in your life where you have a tendency to move out from under authority. How would this ultimately affect your authority? Write down your thoughts. _____

_____

_____

_____

_____

_____

_____

_____

154

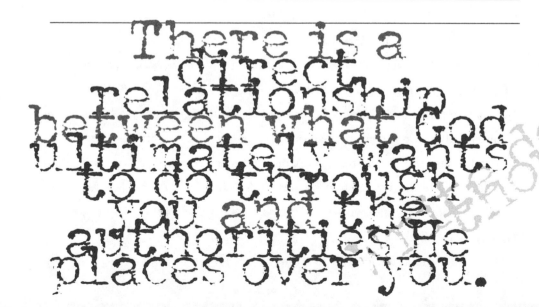

There is a direct relationship between what God ultimately wants to do through you and the authorities He places over you.

Read Matthew 28:18

What scope of authority does Jesus have? _____

_____

_____

_____

_____

How did Jesus get His authority? _____

_____

_____

_____

Who gave it to Him? _____

Think about It

Is it difficult for you to accept that all authority is from God? Why or why not?

_____

_____

_____

_____

_____

Which authorities in your life do you struggle with the most? _____

_____

_____

_____

_____

Day Four
Who's in Charge?

155

Checkpoint #6: Ultimate Authority

Describe some of the consequences you have faced as a result of resisting authority. _____

_____

_____

_____

_____

_____

The idea that all authority is from God is not always easy to accept. What about the father who is in prison? What about the teacher who seems to love to belittle her students? What about the coach who can't stir up his team without shouting profanities?

You can't begin to address all the "what abouts" until you first embrace the truth of God's ultimate authority. You will never be able to deal successfully with unjust or ungodly authorities until you submit to God's control over *all* authority.

The issue is not *what* you are being asked to do. The issue is *who* is doing the asking. This is what I told the students in my youth group:

When someone tells you what to do,

the issue is not *what* but *who*.

Teenagers have a tendency to evaluate rules and requests based upon the merit of the rule or request. If you think a rule or request is reasonable—if it makes sense to you or fits in with your plans or doesn't get in your way—you comply. But if you think that a rule or request is *not* reasonable or *doesn't* make sense or *doesn't* fit in with your plans or *gets* in your way, then you tend to believe it is OK for you to disobey.

This explains why some students can waltz through their front doors at 2:00

A.M. when their curfew was midnight. The rule or request seemed unreasonable and didn't fit in with their plans, so they did their own thing. When their frantic mothers meet them at the threshold, they justify their behavior by attacking the rule or the rule maker. "That's a stupid rule! Mom, you are so unfair!"

Those of us who drive—young and old—often use the same line of reasoning to excuse our traffic violations. "Who put that stop sign there?" "The speed limit is too slow for this road!" In those moments of frustration, it doesn't register in our brains that God established the governing authorities that determine traffic patterns and speed limits. We focus exclusively on the *what* rather than the *who*.

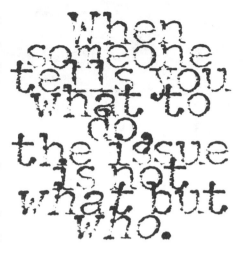

157

As long as your obedience is based on your own evaluation of the rules and requests handed down by those in authority over you, you are retaining control of your life. And as long as you are in control, God is on the sidelines.

But if all the authorities in your life have been put there by God, then *what* you are being asked to do is not as important as *who* is doing the asking. Remember, God ultimately has authority over *all* authority. The question is, Is God going to be in control of your life—or are you?

What do you think about this issue? Ask God to show you deep places in you that might not be in obvious rebellion and record what He says to you.

_____

_____

_____

_____

Day Five
Unjust Authority

158

Read Daniel 1:1–21 and 3:1–30

What was Daniel's response to authority in Daniel 1? _____

_____

_____

_____

Was Daniel *rebelling* against the king's edict or *appealing* it? What is the difference?

_____

_____

_____

_____

In Daniel 3:16–18, what did the "furnace brothers" choose to do? Why? _____

_____

_____

_____

_____

Think about It

Do you trust the primary authorities in your life? Why or why not? _____

_____

_____

_____

_____

_____

_____

_____

What is your normal response when your parents make mistakes while exercising authority over you? _____

_____

_____

_____

_____

Do you think you should cut your parents more slack when they make mistakes?

_____

_____

_____

_____

There are several "facts of life" that complicate the application of the principle "Maximum freedom is found under God's authority." For instance, how do you respond to ungodly authority? Every time I teach on this principle, a handful of students will object based upon the fact that their parents are not believers and therefore are not operating under God's authority. Maybe you or someone you love is in a similar situation.

It is important for you to understand that while not every authority is godly, God establishes every authority—even ungodly authority. Granted, that doesn't make sense on the surface. But the Bible is full of stories that illustrate how God uses ungodly authority to accomplish His purposes. The crucifixion of Christ stands as the paramount example. God's judgment of Israel at the hand of the Babylonians is another good example.

God never sanctions rebellion. Isn't it interesting that Jesus stopped Peter

159

God never sanctions rebellion.

from defending Him against the unjust authorities that came to arrest Him in the garden? The group of priests and soldiers that arrested Jesus acted unjustly and illegally. Yet Jesus refused to rebel or encourage rebellion.

But what about unjust authorities who require those under their authority to participate in actions that are clearly immoral or illegal? What's a believer to do? The Scriptures are filled with examples of men and women who were required by their authorities to do things that were in direct conflict with God's commands. What we find in both the Old and New Testaments are men and women who do two things. First, they address their authorities directly with their intentions not to obey. Second, they willingly accept the consequences. The one notable exception is Daniel.

The story of Daniel provides us with a wonderful model. When faced with a command from the king that went against God's law and Daniel's conscience, Daniel made his intentions clear and signaled that he was willing to accept the consequences. But he also suggested an alternative to the king's edict that was agreeable to those in authority over him. He didn't rebel, and he didn't sin! You too can use this strategy when you are asked or pressured by an authority to do something that you find offensive. Suggest an alternative. It may very well provide you with a way out.

For example, what if your teacher asks your class to do a report on an objectionable topic? Instead of refusing to do the work, you can go to your teacher and suggest an alternative subject. Understand, of course, that if the teacher does not accept your proposal, you must be willing to accept the consequences.

Another option is to appeal to a higher authority—in this case, the principal or department head. Paul modeled this strategy after his arrest in Jerusalem as

160

recorded in Acts 22:25–29. On the basis of his Roman citizenship, he appealed his case to Rome and was spared a mob trial and painful flogging.

The point is that you can find ways to stand up for your convictions without resorting to rebellion. The Bible gives you many good examples. Learn to use these approaches rather than rebel, and you will come to understand what it means to find maximum freedom under God's authority.

What do you think about this? Record your thoughts, needs, and prayers.

_____

_____

_____

_____

_____

_____

161

_____

_____

_____

_____

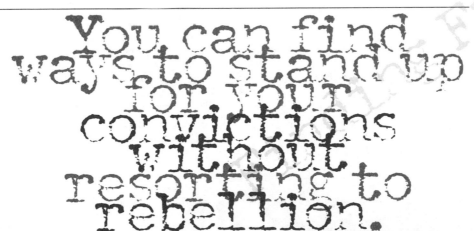

You can find ways to stand up for your convictions without resorting to rebellion.

Day Six
A Command with a Promise

Read Ephesians 6:1–3

According to Paul, why should you obey your parents' authority? _____
_____
_____
_____

Does this passage imply that you should only obey *godly* parents? Why or why not? _____
_____
_____
_____
_____

162

What is the promise connected with the command to obey your parents? _____
_____
_____
_____

Think about It

What do you think the phrase "in the Lord" means in verse 1? _____
_____
_____

In your opinion, what does it mean to "honor" your parents? _____
_____
_____
_____

What do you think it means to have things "go well with you"?_____

_____

_____

_____

_____

_____

Another key insight that must be branded on your heart and mind is this: *To rebel against authority is to rebel against God.* Your attitude and response to the authorities in your life are ultimately your attitude and response to God. You cannot be in rebellion against a God-appointed authority and be in fellowship with God. It's impossible.

If you are rebelling against your parents, it will be hard for you to feel close to God. I can't tell you how many times I have had students come to me burdened by their lack of intimacy with God, only to find out that there is tension and rebellion at home. You can recommit yourself to God time and time again, but your sense of closeness to Him will be short-lived and eventually fade away until you deal with your attitude and response to your parents.

Seeking God's will about something while living in rebellion against authority is futile. You probably have friends who express sincere passion about their relationship with Christ but refuse to come under the authority of their parents. Oftentimes these are the same students who have difficulty discerning God's will when it comes to their choice of friends and their plans for the future.

163

On the other hand, you probably have friends whose spiritual growth suddenly shifted into overdrive when they surrendered to the authorities God had placed in their lives. Looking back, they would agree that the catalyst for their growth spurt was their decision to submit to their parents and acknowledge God's ultimate authority.

To get things right with God, you will have to get things right with Mom and Dad. That simple act of submission to authority can serve as the defining moment for change in your life.

Do you struggle with your parents' authority? What do you need to make right with Mom and Dad? Confess it to God on paper and ask Him to help you submit to their authority in your life. Write it down. _____

_____

_____

_____

_____

_____

_____

_____

_____

_____

164

To get things right with God, you will have to get things right with Mom and Dad.

Read John 8:32

What do you think the Bible means when it talks about freedom? _____

_____

_____

_____

What does Jesus say ensures that you will be free? _____

_____

_____

_____

_____

How do you think this verse applies to the issue of authority? _____

_____

_____

_____

_____

_____

_____

Think about It

Why are freedom and truth closely connected? _____

_____

_____

_____

Day Seven
Responding to Authority

165

Are there any lies or myths that you have believed about authority? Explain.

_____

_____

_____

_____

_____

_____

How do you normally respond to authority? How do your responses *to* authority illustrate what you believe *about* authority? _____

_____

_____

_____

_____

_____

_____

_____

Freedom and God do not mix in the minds of most teenagers. These two entities seem as oxymoronic as saying *poor* Bill Gates or *ugly* Tyra Banks. So when Jesus says that "you will know the truth, and the truth will set you *free*," they may dismiss the simple logic or potential power of such a statement because of *who* made it. "God can't possibly be talking about freedom," they reason, "because He is all about rules and regulations." So students ignore this biblical truth and search longingly for a life with little or no authority, hoping one day to find the elusive land of freedom.

Your understanding of ultimate authority is an important checkpoint because so much of your life is influenced by how you respond to authority. How you respond to God as an authority will have a direct effect on how you respond to your parents. How you respond to parental authority will have a direct effect on how you respond to the laws that govern this land and to the people that enforce those laws. How you respond to the people and institutions that enforce the laws will determine your standing and influence in society.

But this issue is even more personal and deep-seated than this. Your attitude toward authority will ultimately impact your intimacy with God. And it will impact how much authority you are entrusted with.

Marriage is ultimately an authority issue. Parenthood is ultimately an authority issue. Discipleship is ultimately an authority issue. Becoming spiritually influential in the lives of others is ultimately an authority issue.

It may be tempting for you to totally disregard authority and never attach significance to your attitude and response to it. But as you begin to understand how the authority issue influences so many areas of your life, I think you will recognize how important it is for you to submit to the authorities God has placed over you—and to His ultimate authority. True freedom can be found no other way.

Try to make a list of your immediate authorities. Are you rebelling against any of them? Confess, repent, and pray on paper. _____

_____

_____

_____

> Your understanding of ultimate authority is an important checkpoint because so much of your life is influenced by how you respond to authority.

168

Checkpoint #7

Others First
Considering Others before Yourself

Principle

Consider others before yourself.

Critical Question

Are you putting the needs of others ahead of your own?

Key Passage

Philippians 2:3–11

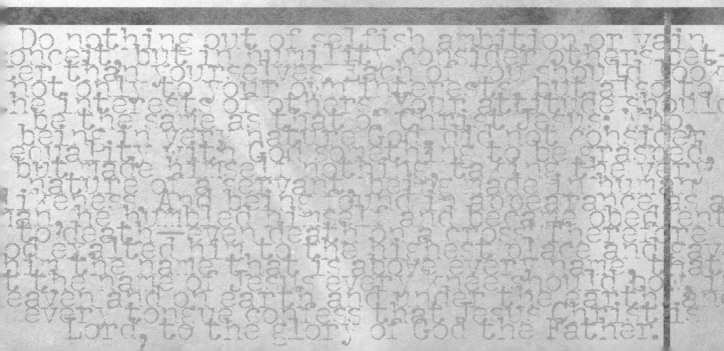

Do nothing out of selfish ambition or vain conceit, but in humility consider others better than yourselves. Each of you should look not only to your own interests, but also to the interests of others. Your attitude should be the same as that of Christ Jesus: Who, being in very nature God, did not consider equality with God something to be grasped, but made himself nothing, taking the very nature of a servant, being made in human likeness. And being found in appearance as a man, he humbled himself and became obedient to death—even death on a cross! Therefore God exalted him to the highest place and gave him the name that is above every name, that at the name of Jesus every knee should bow, in heaven and on earth and under the earth, and every tongue confess that Jesus Christ is Lord, to the glory of God the Father.

Others First
DILEMMA

Monica wants God to be in control of every area of her life, and so far she is succeeding quite well. Monica has a faith that is authentic. She is consistent in spiritual disciplines. She is renewing her mind daily, and it shows. The friends she spends the majority of her time with have the same spiritual desires that she does. Her moral standards are high—so much so that she battles more with loneliness than with the opposite sex. She is making wise decisions based on biblical principles. She is submitting to her parents and the other authorities in her life and is experiencing the freedom God promised.

There is one area, however, that she has yet to allow God to master. Despite her passionate pursuit of God, Monica is often selfish. She battles with the tendency to think of herself first and overlook the needs of others. As a result, she misses opportunities every day to love and minister to peers who really need to see "Jesus with skin on."

Today is no different. As Monica strolls to her locker, immersed in her exclusive Christian world, Brandi stands with her head inside her open locker so that no one can see the tears streaming down her face. The cold darkness of the locker is a perfect mirror of her heart, which is torn by parents who are divorcing and a boyfriend who just decided that his love for her has slipped into the past tense. Monica hears Brandi sniffle and turns just in time to see Brandi's makeup-streaked face push a little farther behind the locker door.

Monica realizes that she is faced with a choice. Should she ask Brandi what's wrong and offer to help? But then she begins to rationalize why she shouldn't get involved. *Brandi's too upset right now. She doesn't want to talk. She doesn't want to talk to me.*

Too late. Brandi slams her locker shut, covers her face with her books, and runs off to her next class.

Monica turns away angry with herself. She's not angry because she missed an opportunity to help. No, what burns Monica like a hot coal is the knowledge that deep down *she really didn't want to help.*

If Monica had been willing to consider Brandi's needs before her own, she would have had an opportunity to show Brandi the loving, forgiving, servant heart of God. Perhaps she would have planted the seed of the gospel in Brandi's needy heart.

Before you are too hard on Monica, you need to look at your own track record when it comes to serving others. Do you consider others before yourself? Becoming selfless is ultimately becoming like Christ. Jesus modeled a life of selflessness. He became a man. He washed His disciples' feet. He went to the cross. Your pursuit of God must intersect with this thought if you are to know God fully and make Him known. Let's talk about it.

171

Day One
A Servant Attitude

Read Philippians 2:5–7

What does Paul mean when he says that Jesus "did not consider equality with God something to be grasped"? _____

_____

_____

_____

_____

Based on this passage, do you think Jesus was born with the heart of a servant or do you think He developed it?_____

_____

_____

_____

Why is the fact that Jesus "made Himself nothing" so amazing? _____

_____

_____

_____

_____

Think about It

Would you consider yourself an extremely selfish person, a somewhat selfish person, or a selfless person? Explain. _____

_____

_____

_____

_____

172

Is your attitude toward serving others the same as Christ's attitude? _____

_____

_____

_____

_____

Do you struggle with ego and pride? Do you think deep down that you are "something"? Be honest! _____

_____

_____

_____

_____

Serving others is not a natural act. You were not born a selfless being. No one who has learned selflessness can look at you and say, "Oh, it comes naturally to me." We all have a bent toward *selfishness*—and that bent is rooted in sin. Because of this bent, serving others has to be an attitude that we develop. We have to be motivated to consider others before ourselves.

The servant attitude we seek is not natural. It's supernatural. And since there is only one supernatural human being who has ever lived—Jesus Christ—we need to look at Christ's life to see how He exemplified the attitude of a servant.

Jesus was equal to God, but He did not consider equality with God something that He needed to hang

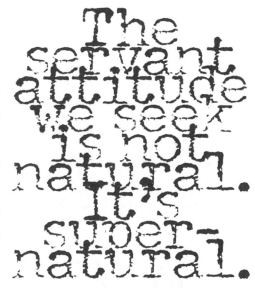

The servant attitude we seek is not natural. It's supernatural.

on to. Jesus wasn't on an insecure "I'm not worthy" trip. But His position was not something so important to Him that He couldn't stand to lay aside. His power was not something so precious to Him that He couldn't go a day without using it.

What *was* precious to Jesus? *People.* Jesus considered people more important than all the power or position in the world. And He wants you to have that same priority.

Is your schedule of activities more important than serving others? Is the position you have among your peers more important than serving others? Is your ego or pride keeping you from stooping to serve?

Jesus *developed* the attitude of a servant. The Bible says that Jesus "*made Himself nothing.*" That puts you on a level field. A servant attitude really is possible! Jesus had to do the same thing that you have to do to serve: make yourself nothing. The difference is that Jesus *was* something and made Himself nothing. You may *think* you are something and have to make yourself nothing. Which do you think is easier?

A servant is someone who lives life as if he or she is nothing. To say that you are "nothing" doesn't mean that you are not worth anything. It is simply a way of expressing your willingness to put others first. The attitude of a servant is the perspective of a heart and mind that says, "My life exists for others."

The paradox is that by living your life as if you are nothing, you become *something* in God's value system. What is your value system? What is worth most to you? If you value *prestige*, you will do the things necessary to gain the admiration of others. If you value *fame*, you will do the things nec-

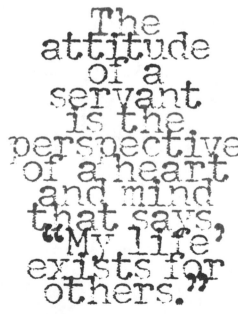

174

The attitude of a servant is the perspective of a heart and mind that says, "My life exists for others."

essary to gain the attention of others. But if you value *people*—if you desire to see them come to know God and grow in their relationship with Him—you will do the things necessary to gain the attitude of a servant.

And in God's eyes, that is something worth dying for!

Are you selfish or selfless? Write down your thoughts on this issue. _____

_____

_____

_____

_____

_____

_____

_____

_____

_____

_____

175

_____

_____

_____

_____

_____

_____

_____

_____

Day Two
Humbling Yourself

176

Read Philippians 2:8

How do you think Paul would define *humility*? _____

_____

_____

_____

_____

What is the significance of Jesus "being found in appearance as a man"? _____

_____

_____

_____

_____

_____

What was the process of humility that Christ went through? _____

_____

_____

_____

_____

_____

Think about It

Do you serve others with a humble heart more times than not? _____

_____

_____

_____

Think of someone in your life whom you know you need to put before yourself. If you were to commit right now to serving that person, what changes would you need to make? _____

_____

_____

_____

_____

_____

What would you be willing to give up to serve that person? _____

_____

_____

_____

Did you hear the one about the person who won the humility contest then bragged about the victory? Humility is a misunderstood concept for most students. You can't proclaim yourself to be humble. You can't really ask others if they think you are humble. Yet God considers humility a trait to be desired and pursued.

Webster defines *humility* as "not proud or haughty; not arrogant or assertive; reflecting, expressing, or offered in a spirit of deference or submission." Holman's Bible Dictionary adds that humility is a "personal quality in which an individual shows dependence on God and respect for other persons." My definition is this: *Humility is a process of determining what is of worth and making yourself nothing to gain what is of worth.*

You probably humble yourself more than you realize. Every time you do something unwise to gain the approval of your friends, you are humbling yourself. Every time you get on the floor to play with a child, you are humbling yourself. Every time you go to work, you are humbling yourself. Having determined that

177

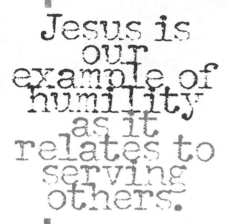

Jesus is our example of humility as it relates to serving others.

something is of worth to you (peer acceptance, a child's happiness, or a weekly paycheck, for example) you are setting aside your own desires—at least for a time—in order to gain that thing.

When Jesus came to earth He became completely human inside and out. Taking on the characteristics of a man was part of the process He went through to make Himself nothing. He set aside His power, His position, and His equality with God to become a servant. He took on the form He needed to take so that He could help the people He considered to be of utmost worth.

Jesus is our example of humility as it relates to serving others. By determining that we were of the utmost worth, Jesus humbled Himself. When you determine that others are of the utmost worth, you too will humble yourself. You will make yourself nothing in order to gain what is best for the people you serve.

Ask God on paper to break you and humble you. Beware! This could change your life. Be honest with God about the areas in your life where pride rules! _____

_____

_____

_____

_____

_____

_____

_____

_____

178

Beware! This could change your life.

Read Luke 9:57–62

What was Jesus trying to communicate to the first man in this story?

_____

_____

_____

_____

What was the meaning of Jesus' answer to the man who needed to bury his

father? _____

_____

_____

_____

Where do you think the third man's heart was? _____

_____

_____

_____

_____

Think about It

Which of these three men are you most like when it comes to priorities? _____

_____

_____

_____

_____

Day Three
Margin
to Serve

179

Checkpoint #7: Others First

When you see an opportunity to serve, do you follow it through or do you have a tendency to start and quit? _____

_____

_____

_____

_____

_____

Make a list of everything that you do and are involved in during the school year. Next make a list of all your gifts and talents (including your spiritual gifts if you know them) as well as what you have a passion to do. We'll come back to these lists in a few moments. _____

_____

_____

_____

_____

Busyness is like a cancer that eats away at the time we have for serving God and others. When we make our schedules, most of us never determine our activities with serving God in mind. As a result, we rarely find time in our week to serve.

Serving God and others doesn't happen by chance. Serving only happens when we make a conscious choice to serve. That is why mission trips become such powerful events in our lives. We make a conscious choice to serve God and others, and through our serving God blesses us.

Serving God and others doesn't happen by chance.

I believe students want to serve God. I believe *you* want to serve God—that's why you're reading these words right now! You may not get involved in serving very often because you think you don't have the time. But you can *find* the time. You just have to properly manage your schedule, your talents, and your resources.

The passage in Luke 10 illustrates how busyness can effect the ability to serve God. Jesus talked with three men who declared their intention to follow him. The first man's heart was full of enthusiasm. The second man's heart held a reservation. "Let me go bury my father" is a Middle Eastern phrase that literally means "Let me attend to my business." The third man's heart was back at home and not really focused on serving Jesus. His "but" got in the way of full-hearted service to God. In each of these situations, busyness was the downfall that kept these men from serving.

Jesus was not implying that service to God requires a reckless abandonment of responsibility to the point of stupidity. Let me be clear:

✔ Jesus doesn't want you to quit school.

✔ Jesus doesn't want you to move out of your home and hate your family.

✔ Jesus doesn't want you to give up your friends.

In fact, you need to be serving God and others in these very environments— at school, at home, and among your friends.

But what Jesus wants is for you to develop "margin" in your life so you'll be available to serve. Margin is that uncluttered, unscheduled space in your life that is available as a reserve to serve. Perhaps you, like most students, are living your life at full capacity physically, mentally, emotionally, and spiritually. This monopoly on your energies robs you of the time and freedom you need to serve God effectively and consistently.

In his book *Margin: Restoring Emotional, Physical, Financial, and Time Reserves to Overloaded Lives*, Dr. Richard Swenson gives the following mathematical definition of margin:

$$\text{Power} - \text{Load} = \text{Margin}$$

Your margin—the time you have to serve—is determined by subtracting your schedule and time constraints from your gifts, talents, and resources. Go back now to the last question in the Think about It section. Based upon your schedule and your gifts, do you have any margin to serve?

Developing margin may call for you to restructure your life somewhat. Ask yourself:

✔ **Is there an activity I need to stop?**

✔ **Is there a relationship I need to give less time to?**

✔ **Are there things that need to be less of a priority?**

Developing and maintaining margin in your life is critical if you want to serve God and others. It is the ultimate antidote to the cancer of busyness.

Are you too busy to serve others? Record your thoughts on this critical issue. Do you have margin? Are you at maximum capacity in all areas of your life?

_____

_____

_____

_____

Read Philippians 2:3–4

Day Four
A Heavenly Hierarchy

What does Paul mean when he says you should *consider* others better than yourself? _____

_____

_____

_____

_____

What do you think he means by "selfish ambition" and "vain conceit"? _____

_____

_____

_____

_____

What does verse 4 say about your purpose in life? _____

183

_____

_____

_____

_____

Think about It

According to these verses, what part of your life can be reserved for just you?

_____

_____

_____

_____

_____

Checkpoint #7: Others First

With the previous thought in mind, why is total selflessness so important when it comes to knowing God? _____

_____

_____

_____

_____

Based on verse 4, do you think that selfishness is ultimately a reflection of your view of *yourself*? Explain. _____

_____

_____

_____

_____

As Christians we have been called to put the needs of others before our own. Too often, however, we end up manipulating others to get what we want. We tend to look at the people around us—with all of their idiosyncrasies and faults—and wonder why we should treat them so specially. We lose sight of the truth that God loved us and served us even when we were unlovable. As a result we feel justified in our "me-first" demands for rights, justice, fairness, payback, and our share of the pie.

When Paul commands you to consider others as better than yourself, you need to understand that he is not saying they *are* better. He is saying you should *consider and treat them* as better. It is easy to see that the world would be a better place if everyone practiced this principle. But since most of the people around you don't put others first, you may think it would be foolish for you to do so. You would get run over, taken advantage of, ignored. You wouldn't get what you deserve. You would be holding the door for everyone who comes along forever. You would be allowing kids to cut in front of you in the lunch line all day.

Right?

What *would* happen if you began to approach all of your relationships from the standpoint of considering others better than yourself? In Christ's hierarchy of values, relationships take precedence over personal rights and due respect. And as His follower you are called to champion, live out, and embrace His values. This is what God wants for you.

Jesus considered others better than Himself, and all of humanity is better for it. What will happen in your little corner of the world if you do the same?

Who do you need to put before yourself? Write down their names and your prayers for them. Record your thoughts and prayers. _____

185

_____

_____

_____

_____

_____

_____

_____

_____

_____

What would happen if you began to approach all of your relationships from the standpoint of considering others better than yourself?

Day Five
A Raging Battle

186

Read James 4:1–3

What does James say is the source of conflict in our lives? _____

_____

_____

_____

_____

Who do you think James is pointing to as the reason for quarrels? _____

_____

_____

_____

_____

Why do we not receive what we ask for? _____

_____

_____

_____

_____

Think about It

Are there any unresolved areas of conflict deep inside you? What are they?

_____

_____

_____

_____

What is the root of each of those areas of conflict? _____

_____

_____

_____

_____

_____

In what areas of your life would you consider yourself selfish? _____

_____

_____

_____

All of us have had our share of quarrels and fighting. As a teenager, you have surely had numerous confrontations with your parents and friends.

James says that the source of these external conflicts with others is an internal conflict that rages within you. There is a battle in you that is erupting from some unresolved conflict, and you can't contain it. Unfortunately the people who are closest to you are the ones who catch the flying shrapnel.

Isn't it interesting that the people you hurt the most tend to be the ones you love the most? So why do you do it? Because there's something going on inside of you, and it's spilling over!

The source of this internal conflict is actually easy to pinpoint: *You can't have your way.* You want something but don't get it, and that frustration looms like an unfulfilled cloud over your bright and sunny day. Maybe you have never identified what it is that you really want, so you live in a constant state of discontent. You're like a ticking time bomb. What do you do when you want something but have no clue what it is? You constantly try to fill that internal hole with external stuff. But you still don't get satisfaction.

Self is never satisfied. Self has an unquenchable appetite. There is not enough

187

C. S. Lewis said that an appetite "grows by indulgence. Starving men may think much about food, but so do gluttons."

stuff, relationships, sex, or whatever else you may desire for self to conclude, "I'm done." The more you feed an appetite, the more it escalates in intensity. In his classic book *Mere Christianity*, C. S. Lewis said that an appetite "grows by indulgence. Starving men may think much about food, but so do gluttons." Ultimately, your appetites and desires are not best dealt with through your attempts to satisfy them.

So what is the solution? *Learn to take your unmet needs and desires to your heavenly Father.* After all, He has promised you abundant life. He has promised to give you more than you can even ask or think. He knows what you need and what will fill that hole in your heart.

Trust God. Say like Jesus, "Not my will, but yours be done." When you do that you give God the option to say no to those things that are not best for you. But that doesn't mean He will always say no!

Lay your internal conflicts to rest at the feet of Jesus. Then—and only then—your external conflicts will cease.

Record what He says to you when you pray that today. _____

_____

_____

_____

_____

Learn to take your unmet needs and desires to your heavenly Father.

Read John 13:2–17

What did Jesus mean when He said, "No servant is greater than his master"?

_____

_____

_____

_____

What did He mean when He said, "Unless I wash you, you have no part of
Me"? _____

_____

_____

_____

_____

According to verse 15, why did Jesus wash the disciples' feet? _____

_____

_____

_____

_____

_____

Think about It

What do you think was the significance of Jesus washing the disciples' feet?

_____

_____

_____

_____

Day Six
Love That
Stoops

189

Checkpoint #7: Others First

Do you think this act paralleled Christ's death on the cross in any way? Explain your answer. _____

_____

_____

_____

_____

Think of the people you will see over the course of the day. How can you symbolically "stoop" to serve them? _____

_____

_____

_____

_____

The act of considering others before yourself holds a power that few notice externally. But the impact of a selfless act echoes deep in the hearts of the one being served and the ones who are looking on. In our world, selflessness is unexpected. By serving others, you not only surprise them with a blessing; you open their hearts to the love and compassion of God exhibited by your service.

At the time of the Last Supper, Jesus had already lowered Himself from His lofty position of equality with God, made Himself nothing, and taken on human likeness. But that night He went even lower. He stripped down from His outer clothing, wrapped a towel around His waist, poured water into a basin, and proceeded to wash the feet of His disciples.

One can only imagine how this act of selflessness confused the disciples. Wasn't Jesus the long-prophesied Messiah? They couldn't believe that their

Master was stooping so low as to take on the servant's job of washing their dirty, stinking feet—while half-naked, no less. What an example of humility!

Love that stoops to serve is unexpected. Your friends expect you to invite them to church and talk to them about Christ. What they don't expect is a love that serves them, a love that seeks their good before your own, a love that goes the extra mile. The ways that you can serve others are countless. The implications of considering others before yourself, however, are clear.

Jesus' reply to Peter looked beyond the act of washing dirty feet to the symbolism Christ intended: Peter needed a spiritual cleansing. Your peers are no different. The real need of their life is not your physical act of serving. But when you consider others before yourself, you actually offer them something more: the grace, mercy, and love of God they so desperately need.

Do you need to love someone radically today? Write down who, what, where, and how. Ask God to anoint your love and selflessness. _____

Love that stoops to serve is unexpected.

191

_____

_____

_____

_____

_____

_____

_____

_____

_____

_____

Day Seven
True Greatness

192

Read Matthew 20:25–28

According to Jesus, what is the connection between greatness and serving? _____
_____
_____
_____

Why did Jesus contrast the rulers and high officials with His disciples? _____
_____
_____
_____
_____

What do you think Jesus meant by saying that in order to be first, you must become a "slave"? _____
_____
_____
_____

Think about It

What clue do we have in this passage that Jesus knew His purpose on earth? What was that purpose? _____
_____
_____
_____
_____

Do you think that "giving [one's] life as a ransom for many" was just Christ's job, or does it have application for us too? _____

_____

_____

_____

_____

_____

How can you give your life as a ransom for many? _____

_____

_____

_____

_____

_____

193

For the past six days you have explored what it means to serve others. You have checked your own life to see how you're doing when it comes to considering others before yourself. You have looked at the attitude of Christ in making Himself nothing and at the process of humility He endured to redeem mankind. Prayerfully you have begun to reserve space in your hurried life to serve others.

You have taken a hard look at the selfishness behind your conflicts with the people around you, and you have recognized the powerful impact that putting others first can have in their lives. Finally, in looking at Jesus' example of washing the disciples' feet, you've learned the ultimate goal of serving.

Greatness in this world comes from many things—power, prestige, wealth, fame. But greatness in the kingdom of God comes only through serving others. It comes only when you learn to stoop to love. It comes only when you humble yourself and consider the needs of others before your own. The principle is true: *When you make yourself nothing, you are really something.*

The battle to consistently consider others before yourself will forever rage. Unfortunately, selfishness is not an enemy that dies and goes away. Self is relentless in its pursuit of its own way, and it seems to lurk just out of view until the timing is right (or wrong). As you pursue intimacy with God, however, the attitude of Christ will become more and more dominant in your life. Selflessness is the by-product of that attitude.

Selflessness will have a positive impact in so many relationships and areas of your life: parents, friends, future spouse, children, school, and work, to name just a few. Ultimately, it will help create in the hearts of those you serve a receptiveness to the grace and love of God.

As you conclude your devotional time, take a few moments to marvel at the selflessness of the one we call Savior and King. Jesus humbled Himself for you and me. We were His singular motivation for emptying Himself of all power and position and taking on the form of a servant. His entire life, death, and resurrection was an act of service to mankind.

Join me now in praying, "Thank You, Jesus, for considering me before Yourself!" _____

_____

_____

_____

_____

_____

_____

Conclusion

Set in Stone
Building a Rock-Solid Foundation

CONCLUSION

In Matthew 7:24–27 Jesus concludes what most consider His most riveting address—we affectionately call it the "Sermon on the Mount"—with an interesting illustration. He likens someone who builds his or her life on biblical truth to a wise builder who builds a house on a rock. When the storms of life come, the house will stand firm because of its rock-solid foundation. But a foolish person does not build his or her life on truth. The picture Jesus gives is of someone who builds a house on a foundation of sand. When storms come, the house will crumble under the pressure of the wind and rain—all because the foundation was flimsy.

As you conclude your forty-nine-day journey through the seven most important principles every teenager needs to know, my prayer is that you are emerging with a rock-solid foundation. These seven checkpoints are the irreducible minimum. They provide a solid foundation of biblically based truth for your life.

What you build on this foundation from this point, however, is up to you. You can either live by these seven principles and build the rest of your life on a rock-solid base, or you can ignore their wisdom, guidance, and instruction, and weather the storms of the teenage years on your own—without an anchor.

Let me echo the advice of Jesus in this passage and encourage you to "hear these words and put them into practice." If you do, this is what you can expect to see happen:

✔ By developing *authentic faith,* you will trust God and walk in absolute confidence that He will do all He has promised to do.

✔ By building your life on *spiritual disciplines,* you will renew your mind and see things the way God sees them. Then you will want to do what God says to do.

✔ By surrounding yourself with *healthy friendships,* you will avoid the pitfalls of unhealthy ones and set a positive direction for a life of quality and depth.

✔ By establishing godly *moral boundaries,* you will live a life of moral purity and pave the way to true intimacy with God and others.

✔ By learning to make *wise choices,* you will walk wisely through the traps and snares of the teenage years. You will also have a decision-making tool that will carry you through the rest of your life.

✔ By submitting to God's *ultimate authority,* you will live a life of freedom and peace under the authorities God has ordained for your life.

✔ By putting *others first,* you will reap the wonderful blessings of identifying with Jesus and serving others the way Christ served you.

197

Living out these seven checkpoints will affect the way you look at your past. It will impact the way you live in the present. It will definitely chart a course for your future. It will impact your relationships with your parents, your friends, those of the opposite sex, your teachers, and everyone else in your world. And it will rivet your life to God—the Father in heaven who loves you and wants what is best for you.

When my family built our home just north of Atlanta, we watched in anticipation as the builders poured the all-important foundation. A huge cement mixer backed up to the mold that had been carefully laid and dumped the wet cement inside its sturdy limits. Then the men worked frantically to make sure every area inside the mold was filled and that the cement was level and smooth. Once they finished, they took a lunch break and left the wet surface to dry.

As soon as they were out of sight, I picked up a stick and walked to the edge of the cement. With strong strokes I wrote my name, the date, and a Bible verse in the drying mixture. I wanted to make sure that my home, in a symbolic yet significant way, was built on a foundation of truth.

For the last forty-nine days, whether you have realized it or not, you've been pouring the foundation for your life. The mold is strong and sure. The cement is wet. Take a minute now—while no one else is looking—and let God carve His name in the foundation. Dedicate your life to Him. Ask Him to make the seven checkpoints a rock-solid base for your life.

And now, I have one final journaling activity for you. This last exercise will be your fiftieth and final day in this book.

God has been under the hood of your life for forty-nine days! He has seen what is up and running in your life, and He has seen what is missing. You have spent time with Him as He inspected those places in you that are so critical to spiritual acceleration and basic function as a Christian.

Let's be honest: Some parts of this journey were painful and frustrating. Others have been encouraging and full of hope!

So now what?

We have provided the following pages to help you pray through what God has shown you over the last forty-nine days. Spend today praying about what you have journaled concerning each checkpoint. Under each checkpoint listed below, record the ways God is encouraging you to apply each principle.

199

#1–Authentic Faith: God can be trusted; He will do all He has promised to do. _____

_____

_____

_____

_____

_____

_____

_____

_____

_____

_____

#2—Spiritual Disciplines: When you see as God sees, you will do as God says. _____

_____

_____

_____

_____

_____

_____

_____

_____

_____

_____

200

_____

#3—Moral Boundaries: Purity paves the way to intimacy. _____

_____

_____

_____

_____

_____

_____

_____

_____

_____

_____

_____

_____

#4—Healthy Friendships: Your friends will determine the direction and quality of your life. _____

_____

_____

_____

_____

_____

_____

_____

_____

_____

_____

#5—Wise Choices: Walk wisely. _____

_____

_____

_____

_____

_____

_____

_____

_____

_____

_____

_____

_____

201

Conclusion: Set in Stone

#6—Ultimate Authority: Maximum freedom is found under God's authority.

_____
_____
_____
_____
_____
_____
_____
_____
_____

#7—Others First: Consider others before yourself. _____

_____
_____
_____
_____
_____
_____
_____
_____
_____

If your time with this journal ends when you close this book, you and I have failed. This is not the end.

This is only the beginning.

What are you waiting for? You have a life to build. Get to work!